Sister

THE SACRED HEART OF JESUS AND THE REDEMPTION OF THE WORLD

Other books by Bernard Häring
Published by St Paul Publications

Hope is the Remedy
Medical Ethics
Faith and Morality in a Secular Age
Sin in the Secular Age
Evangelization Today
Manipulation
Prayer: The Integration of Faith and Life
The Sacraments in a Secular Age
The Beatitudes
The Song of the Servant
The Eucharist and Our Everyday Life
The Sacrament of Reconciliation
Free and Faithful in Christ
Called to Holiness
Christian Maturity

Bernard Häring CSsR

THE SACRED HEART OF JESUS AND THE REDEMPTION OF THE WORLD

St Paul Publications

St Paul Publications
Middlegreen, Slough SL3 6BT, England

First published in Great Britain May 1983
Printed by the Society of St Paul, Slough
ISBN 085439 225 4

St Paul Publications is an activity of the priests and brothers of the Society of St Paul who promote the Christian message through the mass media.

Contents

Acknowledgement
My heartfelt thanks go to Mrs Josephine Ryan for her generous and careful work of polishing up my English and typing the text, and for her constant encouragement during the long time of preparation.

Bernard Häring CSsR

Introduction

ALL humanity, every man and woman, is in dire need of redemption in all its dimensions and at all levels, especially in our innermost self, our heart, which is often wounded, hurt, misdirected, cold, even rigid. But it is our firm belief that even after the fall this inner sensor is neither inert nor mute. Even if evil thoughts, desires, plans and deeds arise from the heart, from its depths comes also a longing, a cry for redemption, for liberty and true love.

It is in the heart that redemption begins to operate and to change the person and the world. Redemption and the healing of persons and their relationships come from God, from his loving designs and "thoughts of peace". They become actual events whenever they touch the human heart with his love.

In the heart of Jesus, the Father's love meets us in incarnate reality and in the most tangible way. From that heart arises the perfect response of human love to the Father. Jesus, who comes from the "bosom of the Father", wants nothing less than to flood our hearts with his own overflowing love, and so to bring us home as participants in the love of the triune God, present and visible in his sacred heart.

The Church, through her devotion to the Sacred Heart of Jesus, wants to awaken us to this liberating truth in order to effect the most profound revolution: the conversion of the human heart, without which there is no effective redemption of the world.

Modern godlessness, is, above all, a perversion of the human heart, man's loss of his centre. Man has gone astray in his inmost being, in his hidden thoughts and desires. This truth, which so deeply touched Blaise Pascal, has to be brought today into the foreground.

"Heart" is a key-concept of humanity. Scarcely any other word recurs so often in Holy Scripture. The holy books of revelation speak of the human heart in a broad scope: as the depth and centre of our being, as conscience, as the inmost calling to love, as being created and recreated for redeemed love. But they also speak of the heart of God who reveals himself simply as Love, in loving deeds and words, in turning his countenance to us and drawing our hearts to himself.

Integrity of heart is the guarantee of healthy human relationships. The word "heart" is both a symbolic and realistic expression for knowing lovingly. We think and speak of the heart especially when "heart finds heart". In everyday language, in popular songs and in literature, attention centres on the heart when a person is deeply moved by the love shown by others or by the Other, and equally if a great love meets rejection or is otherwise distressed.

In the devotion to the Sacred Heart of Jesus, as it has evolved through the centuries and as proposed by the teaching and liturgy of the Church, there is conscious concentration on both the symbolic and palpable reality of the heart, particularly in the personal encounter of our heart with the heart of Jesus.

In this spectrum we come to see and to contemplate the whole of revelation as the dynamic, attractive communication of divine love in and through a human heart that is at the same time divine. And we see also that the noblest vocation of all men and women is to be called to love.

The devotion to the Sacred Heart of our Redeemer is a privileged gateway to true religion — "the cult of love" and "synthesis of the mystery of our religion", as Pius XII expressed it. Its purpose is the triumph of divine love as revealed in the heart of Jesus, a triumph also of God's own love — through his grace in the hearts of the redeemed — over the assaults of hatred, enmity, hardness of heart, terrorism and war. Above all, it is a matter of God's merciful love transforming us in our inmost selves, enabling us to form loving relationship and to be "light for the world".

True veneration of the Sacred Heart of Jesus is the opposite of privatizing religion or indulging in sentimentality. It will be a main purpose of these theological meditations to free it from such misinterpretations.

In the heart of Jesus, Word Incarnate, are revealed the love and mercy of the triune God for all humanity, for the salvation of the world. The divine purpose is nothing less than to bring humankind home to the love of God from which it has gone astray.

It is substantially a matter of the culture of the redeemed who consecrate themselves to the work of redemption in the service of the world. Precisely, it is a call to an all-inclusive solidarity.

The heart of Jesus tells us how great is the love of God for humankind, but also how devastating it is for man's innermost self and for all the world if this love, as revealed and symbolized in the heart of Jesus, is refused. Redemptive love wants to touch and transform us in order to make us light for the world, a new people with healthy relationships.

Inseparable from the devotion to the Sacred Heart is a deeply-felt pain for having offended the all-holy and all-loving God. We all know how much this dimension of repentance needs attention today. Those who are seized by the love of Jesus' heart grieve over the sins of humanity and long for reparation.

This devotion, which for a long time was a great blessing, has diminished during the last decades, at least in some countries. The causes are manifold: coldness of heart, lack of enthusiasm for spiritual realities, enslavement by possessions and consumptions, memories and hearts being drowned in a flood of noise, images and babel in this era of mass media. Frequently, too, it is a case of ignorance or error about the theological foundations of the devotion itself. Every effort to enhance a revival has to take into account these manifold aspects.

Our points of departure here will be Holy Scripture, the Liturgy, and the directives given by the successors of Peter, especially the encyclical *Haurietis Aquas* of Pius XII (1956) which integrates the main lines of thought of his predecessors. It seems important to include also the rich harvest from tradition, from the time of the Church fathers.

Important as the influence of St Margaret Mary Alacoque has been for the devotion to the Sacred Heart and for the development of the respective liturgy, it would be a serious error to think that the devotion started with this seventeenth century saint.

With great fervour the ancient Church fathers meditated and reflected on the wounded heart of Jesus, opened for us even after his death: the "opened port of salvation", "the refuge of sinners", from which spring the Church and all its sacraments, the streams of grace. With holy envy the Church fathers remembered the beloved disciple — the evangelist of love — who at the Last Supper was nearest to the heart of Jesus. This was frequently the context for bringing together the many texts of the Old and New Testaments which tell of the heart-love of God, the image of God as the father of Israel, the divine physician, the good shepherd, the divine spouse who, in spite of all the sins of men, remains faithful to his first love, his people.

St Anselm did much to revitalize this great heritage in his time. St Bernard of Clairvaux had an abiding influence with his deep devotion to the humanity of Jesus and his great love of the Crucified who yearned to draw us all to his heart and thus to the Father. He sees in the heart of Jesus, opened for us, the revelation of the deepest secrets of God, the "thoughts of his heart".

Not less was the impact of St Francis of Assisi and of his order. We look to Francis as the disciple of Jesus, glowing with love, so near to the heart of Jesus that he shared with the beloved Master the wound of his heart and the wounds of his hands and feet. St Bonaventure was a great interpreter of this experience.

The devotion to the Sacred Heart was at its best during the thirteenth century, especially in the monastery of the Benedictine nuns in Helfta, under St Mechtild and St Gertrude the Great. Here the contemplation of Jesus' heart, overflowing with love and drawing all sensitive hearts to himself, was not just casual but became the centre of piety. And here this devotion drew the hearts of many people to a tender love of Jesus.

The Dominican order, too, can claim a good number of fervent promoters of this devotion, beginning with St Dominic himself, and its greatest theologians, from Sts Albert and Thomas Aquinas to the Mystical School of Master Eckehart and Tauler.

The role of Blessed Henry Suso (died 1366) was unique. His love of Jesus' heart, pierced for us all, knew no bounds. As a charismatic poet and preacher he inspired a great number of followers in the same veneration. In his deep devotion to Jesus he combined a feminine and masculine theology. Before him stood Jesus in his full humanity and strength, who made himself humble to heal our tendency to pride. But in his prayers Henry Suso frequently spoke to "divine Wisdom", most loving and most worthy of love. He was overwhelmed by divine Wisdom's love for us, shown in her incarnation and suffering. He exulted when she called him, saying: "My son, give me your heart" (Prov

23:26), "gladden my heart" (Prov 27:11). Enraptured, he responded, "I embrace you with my heart's burning longing". His spirituality was one of constant praise of God's mercy, particularly as revealed in Jesus' suffering heart.

The desired fruit of this loving praise is the gift of such serenity and peace that the disciple of Jesus can feel for suffering people the deepest compassion and the generous love which offers the needed sacrifices.

Henry Suso hears divine Wisdom telling him: "In the great bitterness of my suffering, my boundless love itself is like the sun showing itself in its splendour, like the beauty of the rose in its fragrance, like the mighty fire in its heat. Listen with devotion, therefore, to how much has been suffered for you!" Another time divine Wisdom instructs him: "Through the open wound, enter into my heart wounded for love and lovingly abide and rest in it". Poet and priest, he prays and sings: "Open, O Lord, the shrine of your love; open to me, O Jesus mine, thine heart. Keep my heart free from false love and all its glitter".

Henry tells us also how he gained from divine Wisdom a new understanding of expiation. When he tortured his body in his longing to share in Jesus' loving suffering, divine Wisdom told him gently to stop such nonsense and, instead, abandon himself to the Father's will, calmly accepting all the suffering which the sharing of his love to all people brings with it or requires for the sake of its purity. Once, when he was shamefully defamed, his reaction was: "I shall bring this grievance before Jesus' heart, grieved by love for us". He was grateful that, in the school of suffering, divine Wisdom prepared him for a serene and peaceful conformity with her will. The strength of his love for the loving heart of Jesus was for him also the source of a generous and patient zeal for the salvation of all.

Eckehart's, Tauler's, and especially Henry Suso's writings had a long-lasting influence in France and Italy as well as in Germany. In Italy both the Dominicans and Franciscans promoted the devotion to the Sacred Heart of Jesus, and reached many lay-people, especially through the influence of St Catherine of Siena. In France the influence of these men was deep and lasting, especially through translations of Suso's works. A happy development came about through a synthesis of the mystical approach and the sacramental vision promoted by Cardinal Berulle and his school. It reached a high peak in St John Eudes, the pioneer of the liturgy of the Sacred Heart of Jesus. He wrote liturgical texts for the celebration of the Eucharist and for the breviary in honour of the Sacred Heart, allowed in France by the local ecclesiastical authorities since 1668.

The spirituality and zeal of St Margaret Mary Alacoque for the liturgy of the Sacred Heart follows the same direction as that of St John Eudes. It is not at all a new beginning — as some opponents of this form of devotion thought — but only a new emphasis within a rich tradition with particular interest in its liturgical expression. Its urgent appeal for expiation and conversion to merciful love is characteristic.

Some formulations made by this saint, and especially the ones by those who spread her message, met with considerable opposition and a long-lasting reservation by the Holy See. The authority of St Alphonsus, who himself fervently venerated the Sacred Heart, removed the main obstacle by opposing the theory that the heart is the seat of all affection. His response was that such an assertion cannot at all be proved, is contrary to the insights of science, and in no way necessary for the purpose and meaning of this devotion. In the extensive introduction to his book, *Novena to the Sacred Heart*, he insisted on the basic symbolism of the broader concept of "heart" in the Bible and in tradition. On this basis he gave strong support to the petition of the Polish bishops who, with the Archconfraternity of the Sacred Heart in Rome, had asked for approbation of the public liturgy which was granted by Clement XIII in 1765.

In 1856 Pius IX made the liturgical celebration of the feast of the Sacred Heart of Jesus obligatory for the whole Church. Leo XIII deepened the understanding of the consecration to the Sacred Heart of Jesus and brought into light the relation between the veneration of the Sacred Heart and the salvation of the world.

The crowning and synthesis of the doctrinal development of the devotion to the Sacred Heart is the encyclical *Haurietis Aquas* of Pius XII (1956). By no means does he disown the impulses which came from the humble nun of Paray-le-Monial, St Margaret Mary Alacoque, but insists explicitly that the veneration of the Sacred Heart of Jesus is not based on private revelations but on the Bible and the total tradition.

1

God has first loved us

> "Everyone who loves is a child of God and knows God, but the unloving know nothing of God. For God is love and his love was disclosed to us in this, that he sent his only Son into the world to bring us life. The love I speak of is not our love for God, but the love he showed to us in sending his Son as the remedy for the defilement of our sins. If God thus loved us, dear friends, we in turn are bound to love one another" (1 Jn 4: 8–11).

IT seems to me that a thorough meditation on this first letter of John might be the best introduction to the basic meaning of the veneration of the Sacred Heart of Jesus. As the very first words of the letter indicate, one of the first concerns of this great witness to divine and human love is to share with his readers the most intimate and encompassing experience of love and of the nearness of God in Christ Jesus. "It was there from the beginning; we have heard it; we have seen it with our own eyes; we looked upon it, and felt it with our own hands; and it is of this we tell. Our theme is the word of life. This life was made visible to us. What we have seen and heard we declare to you, so that you and we may share in a common life, that life which we share with the Father and his Son Jesus Christ" (1 Jn 1: 1–3).

In this text the heart of John, who has felt the very beating of the loving heart of Jesus, speaks to us. He testifies that God's own love has made itself visible in the Word Incarnate. It is a tangible love that wants to touch us even in our bodily reality, and especially in that inmost self whose symbol is the pulsating heart. "This is how we may recognize the Spirit of God: every spirit which acknowledges that Jesus Christ has come in the flesh is from God, and every spirit which does not thus acknowledge Jesus is not from God" (1 Jn 4: 2–3).

The heart of Jesus, whose pulsation was felt first by his mother when she bore him in her womb and which lived and suffered for all of us, the heart whose anguished concern for us bathed Jesus' body in a blood-sweat and was pierced by the soldier's lance even after he had died for us: this heart best symbolizes and synthesizes the central truth of our faith in the incarnation of the Son of God.

In this most sensitive human heart the love of the Father and for the Father burned and radiated. It loved the Father perfectly in the name of all creation. And it is in this heart that we see the love by which the Father has loved us.

With Johannine affection Cardinal Newman addresses Jesus: "My God, my Saviour, I adore thy sacred heart, for that heart is the seat and source of all thy tenderest human affections for us sinners. It is the instrument and organ of thy love. It did beat for us. It yearned for us. It ached for us and for our salvation. It was on fire through zeal that the glory of God might be manifested in and by us. It is the channel through which has come to us all thy overflowing human affection, all thy divine charity towards us. All thy incomprehensible compassion for us, as God and man, as our creator and redeemer and judge, has come to us, and comes in one inseparable mingled stream, through that sacred heart. O most sacred symbol and sacrament of love, divine and human, in its fullness thou didst save me by thy divine strength and thy human affection, and then at length by that wonder-working blood, wherewith thou didst overflow".

In the heart of Jesus, most loving and willing to suffer for love's sake, creation and the history of salvation find their ineffable centre and summit. Gratefully contemplating this heart, we understand in a wholly new way that God created world and man for no less a purpose than to have sharers of his own blissful love.

In the heart of the Son there is the unsurpassable reality of sharing in the Father's love and in the power of the Spirit of truth and love. In this perfect spectrum and symbol, divine and human love are brought together. The love of the Father flows to his Son and, in him and through him, to humankind; and the purest human love, the authentic love of humankind, flows to the Father from the heart of the Son.

For God, who is love in triune fullness, there would be no motive for the creation of humankind other than his overflowing love, his total freedom to share his love and to call us to this sharing. He wants us, his people, not just as recipients of his love but as concelebrants, joyous sharers of the very love with which the Father loves the Son and the Son responds to the Father in the mutuality of the Spirit. This touches the most profound meaning of the word that God created man and woman in his own image and likeness.

The more we respond to God's love and his call to return love, and the more zealously we learn what it means to love Jesus and with Jesus, the more we become a mirror-image of God in reality and truth. Here on earth we are learners in the best sense when we learn, in and from the heart of Jesus, to love the Father and to share in his and Jesus' love for all people. The final goal is the eternal feast of love with God in the communion of saints.

Sinful man locks himself up in his perverted self-love, in the loveless fortress of self-defence. All sins are marked by lovelessness, by the decreasing capacity to discern what true love is and to strive for nothing less. Utter lovelessness is godlessness, having no share in God who is love. What some scientists imagine about a final dissolution of the world through a kind of loss of energy is only a pale image of a world frozen in lovelessness.

Praise be to God that in his great love he remains faithful to his design! Despite the sinfulness of humankind, he follows "the decision of his heart" (Jer 30: 24). Only a heart of stone will not be moved by hearing God's word: "I will love them with all my heart; I will heal their disloyalty" (Hos 14: 5).

Faithful to the thoughts of his heart, God has sent his beloved Son as redeemer of rebellious mankind, and to fulfil this mission by the strength of his merciful love. As believers, our response can be only amazement, praise and unlimited gratitude. Our wonder will never cease when we meditate on the words: "The Word became flesh; he dwelt among us, and we saw his glory, such glory as befits the Father's only Son, full of grace and truth. . . . No one has ever seen God; but God's only Son, he who is nearest to the Father's heart, he has made him known" (Jn 1: 14–18).

That he "who is nearest to the Father's heart" has come in the flesh to make known the love of the Father is, since apostolic times, what has inspired the veneration of the heart of Jesus, whose love comes from the Father and leads to the Father.

It is not enough to see Jesus as the model, prototype and

object of our love. There is more. He has come to share with us his own love for the Father and the Father's love for us. He unites our hearts with his own when we open ourselves to him in faith and trust. By his Spirit, Christ enables us to grasp "God's secret. That is Christ himself; in him lie hidden all of God's treasures of wisdom and knowledge" (Col 2 : 2–3).

Paul's gospel is that we believers have "life in Christ Jesus". Hence, he urgently appeals: "Live your lives in union with him. Be rooted in him; be built in him; be consolidated in the faith you were taught; let your hearts overflow with thankfulness" (Col 2 : 6–7).

A heart touched by the heart of Jesus is, indeed, "overflowing with thankfulness". This is the constant, joyful acknowledgment that God has first loved us, and that the love he has manifested to us in Jesus is utterly undeserved and cannot dwell in ungrateful hearts. One of christianity's oldest songs of praise, which comes to us in the introduction of Paul's letter to the Ephesians, expresses thankfulness for the amazing graciousness of God's revelation in Jesus. "Praise be to the God and Father of our Lord Jesus Christ, who has bestowed on us in Christ every spiritual blessing in the heavenly realms. In Christ he has chosen us before the world was founded, to be dedicated, to be without blemish in his sight, to be full of love; and he destined us — such was his will and pleasure — to be accepted as his children through Jesus Christ, in order that the glory of his gracious gift bestowed on us in his beloved, might redound to his praise" (Eph 1 : 3–6).

For the Apostle of the gentiles, ingratitude, insensitivity and hardness of heart are marks of "misguided minds plunged in darkness" and of a perverted culture (Rom 1 : 21–28).

In Jesus' warnings about the eschatological birth-pangs, he points to the greatest evil: "As lawlessness spreads, men's hearts will grow cold" (Mt 24 : 12). In the New Testament "lawlessness" is, above all, lack of love, the total refusal of the liberating law of love that Jesus has granted us.

In a decisive religious experience, St Margaret Mary Alacoque saw Jesus painfully shaken by the coldness of so many hearts and because so few people were moved to honour his heart by their own thankfulness and fervent love in compensation for the wounds inflicted by this thanklessness. When the saint complained to the Lord about her own incapacity, such a flame of love came from the heart of the glorified Lord that she was afraid of being burned by its fire. But Jesus told her: "I shall be your strength".

The meaning of this symbolic experience is central to the devotion to the Sacred Heart. It calls for: abiding gratitude for God's initiative in revealing his love to us through Jesus' heart pierced for us and his blood shed for us; faith-filled trust that the heart of the risen Christ will never stop beating with love for us; a great longing to see Jesus praised by all and receiving from us a response worthy of such a great love; and finally, a fervent longing to atone, by ever greater love and gratitude, for our earlier neglect and for all offences against the loving heart of Jesus. We yearn to see our love purified and strengthened, united with the love of Jesus and of all his true disciples, so that Jesus' love will be felt by ever more people. And we want our hearts to be so filled by Jesus' own love that, through us, the love of God and of Jesus may reach many hearts.

In the liturgy in honour of the Sacred Heart of Jesus, renewed in 1928, we hear again Jesus' urgent invitation: "If anyone is thirsty, let him come to me; whoever believes in me, let him drink" (Jn 7:37–38).

Those who truly venerate the Sacred Heart are longing not only to refresh themselves at the fountain of salvation; they thirst, above all, to see God loved and honoured by everyone. For the loving disciples of Christ the danger of a deadly coldness in so many hearts is frightening. They are willing to do everything in their power to draw others to the same love of the heart of Jesus so that they, too, may be transformed by it.

Our present technically developed humanity is in great danger of losing life's centre, the inner resources of people's hearts, and thus losing the wholeness of vision. In this threatening situation we cannot fail to promote the veneration of the Sacred Heart. In his encyclical *Miserentissimus Redemptor* Pope Leo XIII said a word of lasting relevance: "In the Sacred Heart of Jesus we are given a symbol of the unchangeable love of Christ which, by itself, moves us to the response of love".

* * *

"Father, we rejoice in the gifts of love
we have received from the heart of Jesus, your Son.
Open our hearts to share his life
and continue to bless us with his love".

(Liturgy of the Sacred Heart)

2

God's love knows no bounds

> "It was before the Passover festival. Jesus knew that his hour had come and he must leave this world and go to the Father. He had always loved his own who were in the world, and now he was to show the full extent of his love" (Jn 13 : 1).

> "There must be no limit to your goodness, as your heavenly Father's goodness knows no bounds" (Mt 5 : 48).

THE central truth of revelation is "God is love". This concerns not only the innermost life of the triune God but is also the good news about God's relationship with the created world and especially with humankind.

Indeed, God has gone to utmost limits to make known to us his infinite love in a way that touches our heart, mind and will. He speaks the language of the heart flowing from the heart of Jesus, pierced for us, and sends us his Holy Spirit so that our hearts can become sensitive, affectionate, grateful for his sublime love.

God speaks to us through all of creation. In its beauty and bounty it is an assurance of God's overflowing, attractive love. Heaven and earth sing the praise of the creator, who reveals his perfection and majesty in all his works. It belongs to the essence of beauty that it speaks to the whole person, inviting admiration, reverence and praise. A heart sensitive to beauty cannot but wonder: if the beauty of the created reality fills our hearts and minds with delight, how much more glorious must be the beauty of the creator!

When a person's countenance becomes particularly beautiful — when he or she receives love and responds to it — our hearts exult, knowing that this is a wonderful reflection of God's own countenance turning to us in boundless love. The hearts of parents beat with joy on seeing the smile of their child — which in itself is an amazing response to the love the child has received from them. Only a fool can fail to discover that all this arises from God, our creator, and invites our response to his gracious love.

Yet this is only a prelude to the supreme revelation of God's love in the incarnation, life, death and resurrection of his only Son. Creation by the eternal Word is already a fascinating message from the Father. He has created the world in the same Word in whom he eternally speaks out all his being and all his love. But even more wonderful is the event that the Father sends us this Word in the flesh of the world, our own humanity, to be for us "Emmanuel — God-with-us", "Son of Man", "One-of-us". The Word Incarnate, the "One-of-us", is the supreme investment not only of God's might but, above all, of his eternal love in the created world.

God, our creator, is also the supreme artist, making us into his own image, awakening us to the revelation of his love and gracing us with the will to respond to it with all our being, our heart, memory, mind and will. In the Word Incarnate, God has become also our brother, "one-of-us", our dearest friend, our saviour, our divine physician. Holy Scripture uses even the most intimate image: God, the "spouse" of his people; Jesus, the "spouse" of his Church and, indeed, of all redeemed humankind.

God speaks his love to us, addresses our heart and mind through his own substantial Word who eternally breathes the Spirit of love. But our amazement is not ended. In his Incarnate Word, God enters into our deepest human misery, except sin; yet he takes upon himself the burden of our sin-solidarity. As "one-of-us" he becomes one with the poor, the oppressed, the outcast, so that he may bring us home into the riches and honour of redeemed love. No earthly wealth or comfort should let us forget that he is the revelation of divine love and the one who, in the name of all the universe, gives to the Father the full response of boundless love, drawing us to his heart so that we may join him in this response.

The divine "one-of-us" who is "God-with-us" takes our misery so much to heart that, bearing our anguish and estrangement, he sheds his blood on the cross. Fully aware of his divine origin and his returning into his own in the glory of the Father, Jesus says his unsurpassable, self-giving "yes" to atoning love. Facing the naked unbelief and hatred embodied in the ruling religious class, he reveals the full extent of God's boundless love.

Surely, God did not set in motion the murderous assault on his beloved Servant and Son, Jesus. But in full knowledge of the abyss of human sinfulness, Father and Son, in the loving power of the Spirit, took this unique risk. Jesus did not come just as leader of salvation-solidarity for his own. If sinful man, sinful leaders, and seducers of the people would really go that far in their callousness and blindness, the "Son of Man", the "One-of-us", would not shy away from this hideous pit of sin-solidarity. He goes all the way to drink the bitter dregs of the chalice of suffering.

Full of wonder at this unsurpassable ardour of God's love, Paul writes: "He did not spare his own Son, but gave him up for us all; and with this gift how can he fail to lavish upon us all he has to give?" (Rom 8:32). By "all he has to give", Paul means the absolute assurance of the victory of God's love. He had experienced it in his own conversion and election. "Then what can separate us from the love of Christ? . . . I am convinced that there is nothing in death or life, in the realm of the spirits or superhuman powers, in the world as it is and in the world as it shall be, in the forces of the universe, in heights or depths — nothing in all creation that can separate us from the love of God in Christ Jesus our Lord" (Rom 8:35–39).

St Alphonsus, like many other theologians, was faced time and again with the question of whether the Son of God could atone for our sins only by suffering the terrible death on a cross. He came to the firm conclusion that this cannot be, even in view of the horrible history of human sinfulness. All that the Incarnate Word did on earth would have been sufficient for atonement, since it was done with infinite love. For St Alphonsus and other doctors of the Church the decisive reason was that God wanted there to be no limit to the revelation of his love.

In a profound, heartfelt experience, we all should realize that the goodness and nearness of God know no bounds. Divine and redeeming love should manifest its victory at the very abyss of human deprivation. This is the power of the love that inflamed the sacred heart of Jesus. Through it God wanted to speak to our hearts: "What more could I, in my great love, do for you?"

The beloved disciple, who was nearest to the heart of Jesus at the Last Supper, introduced the farewell discourses and the high-priestly prayer spoken there, with the words: "He was to show the full extent of his love" or, as some translate: "He loved them utterly to the end" (Jn 13:1). This refers to the bitter suffering and death which Jesus foresaw and which he accepted as the Father's will. But we may think also of the Eucharist which, on that occasion, was given as a testament to his disciples, as an abiding memorial for grateful memories.

Jesus' utter self-giving, "making himself nothing, assuming the nature of a slave" (Phil 2:7) in his incarnation, life, suffering and death, continues in another mysterious way in the Eucharist. This is an essential feature in the self-revelation of the Word of God. So much has Jesus bound himself to us weak human beings in his incarnation and suffering that, even after his death and resurrection, he wants to give us the most explicit sign of remaining "one-of-us", a total gift to us of his abiding presence.

The institution of the Eucharist at the Last Supper coincides with the solemn promise to send us the Holy Spirit. In the power of the Spirit Jesus has given himself up for us. In the same power he makes a gift of himself to us in the Eucharist and enables us, through the Spirit, to surrender ourselves to him. In granting this wonderful memorial he wants to change our forgetfulness into a grateful, loving memory.

In all this, Jesus speaks to our hearts, especially if we contemplate it with our eyes and our minds fixed on his own sacred heart, pierced for us, opened to shower streams of grace upon us. In the presence of the risen Lord in the Eucharist, we know that his heart will never stop beating for us.

* * *

O heart of Jesus, most worthy of adoration, glowing with love for us who are created for this very love, how is it possible that you find so poor a response from people, even to the point of disregard? I, too, in my misery, once belonged to the thankless ones and did not know how to love you. Forgive me, my Jesus, this great sin of having refused my love to you who, by your own love, urged me to respond with a grateful heart. By withholding my love I would deserve the terrible punishment of being unable to love you. My beloved Redeemer, spare me this punishment. Compared with it, any other punishment would be small. Grant me the grace to love you; then I shall have no fear. Yet how could I fear such a terrible infliction, since I know that you continue to share with me your blissful commandment: "Love the Lord with all your heart"?

Yes, O my God, you want to be loved by me, and I want nothing more than to love you who have loved me so much. O heart of my Jesus, you are my love. O heart glowing with love, inflame my heart with love for you.

Keep me in your love for all my life, so that there will never be a moment when I live without loving you. Let me rather die than show the world such thanklessness as to disown again your holy love. Never, O Jesus, never let this happen! I put my trust in your precious blood, shed for me, and hope that I shall love you, and you love me, forever: that this love between us will last forever.

Mary, Mother of our Beautiful Love, you yearn to see your Son loved; bind me so firmly to him with the bond of love that I will never be severed from him.

(Prayer of St Alphonsus in *Novena to the Sacred Heart*)

3

Love calls for love

"I have come to set fire to the earth, and how I wish it were already kindled! I have a baptism to undergo, and what constraint I am under until the ordeal is over!" (Lk 12:49).

JESUS knows all too well the tremendous obstacles opposing his mission to set humanity free for redeemed and redeeming love. He has come from the Father to kindle the fire of true love. His heart is aflame with love and with the desire to see the Father loved by all people. His yearning to enkindle us with the fire of his own love is greater than the constraint with which he awaits the coming ordeal of death on the cross.

The heart of Jesus, pierced by man's lovelessness, yet opened as the fountain of love for us, perfectly symbolizes the truth that he who *is* love calls for love. The all-loving God wants to be loved by us.

The essence and dynamics of true human love require a response in love. Anyone who is not interested in this love-response can hardly claim that he really loves. Jesus calls for our response of love. We may even say he "courts" it by the efficacious means of communicating his love to us. He knows that we cannot enter into the eternal feast of the triune love unless we learn here on earth to love our creator and redeemer. The blood-baptism which he foresees and accepts is, indeed, anguishing; but since it should become the sign of our blood-brotherhood with him, he awaits the great hour when it will be consummated on the cross.

Jesus prays: "Father, shall I say, 'Save me from this hour?' No, it was for this that I came to this hour. Father, glorify your name". And the voice, like thunder, resounds from heaven, "I have glorified it, and I will glorify it again". The privileged hour in which the name of the Father is glorified is the terrible hour —

the three hours — of Jesus' agony on the cross. By his great love and trust Jesus glorifies the name of the Father, and the Father glorifies his Son by this victory of love.

Jesus explains to his disciples an essential aspect of this glorification of the Father's name: "I shall draw all men to myself when I am lifted up from the earth". One might think that this "lifting up" refers exclusively to Christ's resurrection, but the evangelist makes clear what Jesus meant: "This he said to indicate the kind of death he was to die" (Jn 12:27–33).

O holy cross, sign of torture, now you have become the sign of redeeming love! The voice of the Father tells us what you mean for him and for us. You recall to our hearts through all the ages how much the heart of Jesus thirsts for our love, so that the name of the Father of all will be glorified.

Jesus' being lifted up on the cross is the first act of an indivisible drama. Lifted up to heavenly glory, Jesus sends us the Holy Spirit to draw us to his heart which forever glorifies the Father, while manifesting his love for us and calling for love in return. He tells us that the Father, too, desires our love and a loving knowledge of his name. "No one can come to me unless he is drawn by the Father who sent me" (Jn 4:44). The call for our love in return for love, united with Jesus' love, is the work of the whole Trinity.

Already in the Old Testament God speaks the language of love calling for love in return. "I myself taught Ephraim to walk, I took them in my arms; yet they have not understood that I was the one looking after them. I led them with reins of kindness, with leading-strings of love. I was like someone who lifts up an infant close against his cheek; stooping down I gave him his food" (Hos 11:3–4). Like many other texts, this reminds us that the most tender love of a human heart is a God-given experience which should lead us to an ever deeper understanding of God's own love, the source of all human affections.

Eternal Wisdom calls: "My son, give me your heart" (Prov 23:26). God wants us whole and wholly. His love wants to touch us, to move us in our depths, to take hold of us and set us free for the full sharing of his own blissful love. We have to make the decision, and by opening ourselves to his love and grace we are able to do so. "No one can be slave to two masters" (Mt 6:24).

If we make up our mind to seek first and above all else the kingdom of God and its saving justice (Mt 6:33), then we begin to savour the word of Jesus: "Where your treasure is, there will be your heart also" (Mt 6:21). God will give us a wholly new understanding of his love, an ever-increasing joy of being seized by his love and called to intimate union with him. When we strive for nothing less than to love God with all our heart, then we are becoming "adorers of God in spirit and truth".

In Jesus, God shows himself thirsting for our love-response, since he himself is overflowing love and the centre of all creation, but also because only in this full response of love can we ourselves find the sense and purpose of our life, our completion and our abiding joy.

God cannot accept a superficial, divided love as worthy of his majesty. Of this truth we are constantly reminded by the divine commandment: "Listen Israel: Yahweh your God is the one Yahweh. You shall love Yahweh your God with all your heart, with all your soul, with all your strength. Let these words I urge be written on your heart" (Deut 6:4–6).

If this gracious commandment is written in our hearts, then we understand it as an appeal coming from the pierced heart of Jesus, and we can only wonder how anyone could ever refuse response to such an amazing love. How can we, who have been redeemed, ever cease rejoicing at this invitation to love our Saviour? Captured by the love of Jesus and by his zeal for the glory of the Father, his disciples will yearn with him to see the Father loved by all. And this will be an added incentive for greater zeal for the love of neighbour whom the Father has created.

The thought that so many saints in heaven and on earth have dedicated themselves to respond to God's love in union with the sacred heart of Jesus is an invitation to joy and praise. "Shout for joy, daughter of Zion, Israel shout aloud! . . . Yahweh your God is in your midst. He will exult with joy over you, he will renew you by his love" (Zeph 3:14–17).

This rejoicing of God, while renewing our hearts with his love, must not be misunderstood as his needing our love-response for his own fullness of beatitude. He does not love us out of a need for bliss but out of the superabundance of his own love and his design to make us sharers of his eternal feast of love. His joy in our response is simply a part of that love. The Sacred Heart of Jesus is the abiding symbol of this truth.

The insight that the all-holy God does not need our love has led some theologians — Emil Brunner, for instance — to draw the false conclusion that God is not interested in being loved by us. What he wants, they say, is that we turn our love to our neighbour and so give thanks for God's love. Such a theory contradicts the central truths of revelation and of basic human experience. What loving parent would say to his children: "I am not interested in your responding to my love for you; I want only that you love others"? Such strange thinking would also undermine the love of neighbour. How can a person whose parents have no interest in his or her love-response be a loving brother or sister?

Jesus wants to draw us to his heart, and the Father draws us to Jesus and himself. While doing so, God offers us a new heart, enabling us to join him in his feast of love and his love for all mankind.

The tradition of the devotion to the Sacred Heart expresses this truth in various images. St Albert the Great, with Sts Gertrude the Great and Mechtild, speaks of an "exchange of hearts". We renounce our selfish love and allow Jesus to rid us of it in order that we may be fully inserted into his holy love. Thus Jesus can dwell in our hearts, and we are at home in his loving heart. For that we pray: "Jesus, touch our hearts and make them like your own!"

This is also clearly expressed in the Johannine and Pauline theology of "life in Christ Jesus". Filled with love of Christ, the Apostle of the gentiles can exult: "The life I live now is not my life but the life which Christ lives in me" (Gal 2:20).

We venerate St Francis of Assisi who was so thoroughly inspired with love of Jesus Crucified that he was found worthy by Jesus to be impressed with the wound of his pierced heart. The life of St Francis and of many other saints tells us one thing: Love calls for love! God the Father, who has called us through the love of Jesus, is truly interested in our response of love. Nothing is more urgent than loving God "with all our heart". This is the decisive message from the saints, who tell us also that with God's grace this is possible.

If we live consciously and gratefully according to the grace and message of baptism, confirmation and the Eucharist, we shall realize ever more that we, too, are marked by the heart of Jesus, pierced for us, sealed by his precious blood and that through the gift of the Spirit we are truly invited to return love for love.

* * *

My dear Saviour, I say with St Augustine: you command me to love you and threaten me with punishment if I do not love you. But what more horrifying punishment, what more terrible disgrace can there be than to be deprived of your love? If, then, you want to frighten me, threaten only that I would have to live without loving you, and this will frighten me more than the threat of hell. If, in the midst of hell's flames, the condemned could be inflamed with your love, hell would become paradise. And if, on the other hand, the blessed in heaven were unable to love you, paradise would become hell.

My beloved Lord, I realize that by my sins I have deserved to be deprived of your grace and condemned not to love you; but I know that you still tell me to love you, and I feel a great desire to do so. This desire is your own gracious gift. Give me, then, also the strength and fidelity to put this into practice. Help me, so that now and forever I can truthfully and with all my heart repeat: "My God, I love you. You desire my love and I desire yours".

Forget then, O Jesus, the displeasure I have caused you in the past. Love calls for love. I shall not abandon you; you will never abandon me. Forever you will love me and forever I shall love you. My dear Saviour, I put my trust in your merits. Allow a sinner, who has so gravely offended you, to love you.

Immaculate Virgin Mary, assist me; pray Jesus for me.

(Prayer of St Alphonsus in *Novena to the Sacred Heart*)

4

God loves us sinners — me, a sinner

> "For at the very time when we were still powerless, then Christ died for the wicked. Even for a just man one of us would hardly die, though perhaps for a good man one might actually brave death; but Christ died for us while we were yet sinners, and that is God's own proof of his love towards us. And so, since we have now been justified by Christ's sacrificial death, we shall all the more certainly be saved through him from final retribution. For if, when we were God's enemies, we were reconciled to him through the death of his Son, how much more, now that we are reconciled, shall we be saved by his life! But that is not all: we also exult in God through our Lord Jesus, through whom we have now been granted reconciliation" (Rom 5:6–11).

IN the course of a cruel battle in Russia during the Second World War, when many medical orderlies had been lost, I heard calls for help from a neighbouring unit. In spite of extreme exhaustion, I ran to look for the wounded man. He was in hopeless condition. After a first aid I told him, "I am a priest", and asked if he would like to receive the sacraments, including holy communion. When he heard this, there was a sudden change. Astonished and with great joy he said over and over: "How is this possible that the Lord shows such great love for me, a sinner!". Because of a sad conflict with a parish priest, this otherwise good man had left the Church but felt great sorrow about it. And now he had proof that God had not abandoned him. His gratitude was so great that he seemed almost to forget his terrible pain, and death did not frighten him anymore.

None of us should be less astonished or less grateful when we realize that God loves us sinners — me, a sinner — so much that he calls for my love in return.

This amazement and grateful love marked the whole life and activity of the Apostle of the gentiles. Each new benefit and even each occasion to share in Christ's suffering reminded him of what a sinner he had been when the Lord chose and called him. This experience increased his zeal for the gospel of reconciliation and helped him to bring many people to this same sense of marvel and of thankful love for Jesus.

The wonder that God so loves *us* sinful people does not really penetrate us unless we are touched by the experience that God loves *me*, the sinner, so much that he calls for my love in return.

Many of the Pharisees were shocked that Jesus showed such great love and kindness to tax collectors and to persons of ill-repute. They were scandalized and angry because it did not enter their minds that they, too, had no title whatsoever to be loved by God except through his own merciful love. Indeed, the arrogant conviction that one has merits and claims for God's love is one of the most abhorrent sins against God's undeserved love for us: a sin that locks man's heart against this very love.

When the woman who was an object of public contempt began to show signs of sincere and humble love for Jesus, he welcomed that love, since it came from a contrite and grateful heart. And his acceptance gave her the trust that she could continue to grow in grateful and humble love. "Her great love proves that her many sins have been forgiven; where little has been forgiven, little love is shown" (Lk 7:47). This last assertion is a strong warning for those who think that they are not really in need of divine mercy and forgiveness.

The saints are so touched by the healing love of God, and so filled with awe before a God who loves "me, a sinner", that they are scarcely tempted to ponder their own sins by looking down on others as greater sinners. Rather, they compare their sins with the love of the all-holy God whom they have offended. Before him our sins have their weight in view of the many signs of grace by which he calls us to return his love. Before God every boast about merits is simply excluded; there is place only for wonder and humble praise.

This wonder and praise mark the lives of the saints, particularly those who are great promoters of the devotion to the Sacred Heart of Jesus. We see it, for instance, in the prayers of St Margaret Mary and, perhaps still more, in those of St Alphonsus in his book *Novena to the Sacred Heart*. Like other theologians,

St Alphonsus speaks in his writings on the subject of merits under the influence of grace, but in his prayers he never speaks of merits. Speaking to God, he simply could not think about his own merits, since he was wholly filled with amazement that God so much loves us who sin against him.

The contrition to which the Church ascribes justifying power is not just a vague kind of sorrow for our sins but a deep and painful grief for having offended a God who loves us so tenderly and mercifully. The word "mercy" (cf. the Latin *misericordia*) concerns a loving heart for those in misery, while the "miser" has no heart for those who are in need. God's heartfelt love for us sinners, who are so much in need of compassion, finds its striking symbol in the pierced heart of Jesus.

The marvel that God loves *me*, a sinner, forges bonds of a solidarity of salvation. If God loves me, how much must I then praise him for loving all of us together who are sinners. Thus we are joined in his praise and in mutual compassionate love.

The tears of compassion in contemplating the unspeakable suffering of Jesus for us sinners — for me — melts our pride and frees us from fruitless self-pity. Our love-response to Christ, crucified by us and for us, joins us in his compassion for all of us. If our hearts become thus conformed to the heart of Jesus, we then become, all together, compassionate, warm-hearted and generous disciples of Christ. Our gratitude and awe will lead to zeal for the salvation of all.

This truth is touchingly expressed in the story of the calling and conversion of Matthew (Mk 2: 14–18). As soon as Matthew (Levi), the tax-gatherer, was called to follow Jesus in intimate friendship, he prepared for Jesus a festive meal to which he invited many other people like himself. "When Jesus was at table in his house, many tax-collectors and sinners were seated with him and his disciples" (Mk 2: 15), to the great scandal of some doctors of the law. Evidently the humble heart of the newly converted Levi told him: "I am no better than other sinners. If the Master invites me, then all are invited". Thus Jesus celebrates the messianic meal of the redeemed.

We find a similar experience of awe and amazement in the context of Peter's election. "Go, Lord, leave me, sinner that I am!" (Lk 5: 8). Surely Peter does not want to be abandoned by Jesus, but in his astonishment at being chosen he realizes how unworthy he is of the friendship and nearness of Jesus. This experience reaches still greater depth and purification when, after his thrice repeated denial of his Master, the risen Christ asks him three times about his friendship. The marvel, "So much does the Lord love me, unworthy sinner", vitalizes his confirmed ministry as shepherd in the steps of the Good Shepherd.

In the Bible we find other instances of how one's humble amazement — that God calls "a sinner like me" to proclaim the message of salvation — sparks the readiness to shoulder a difficult mission. At first, Isaiah cries out: "What a wretched state I am in! I am lost, for I am a man of unclean lips and I live among people of unclean lips, and my eyes have looked at the King, the Lord of hosts" (Is 6: 5). After being touched by the purifying fire of God's holy love, he hears the Lord saying: "Whom shall I send?" and he answers: "Here I am; send me" (Is 6: 8).

Deutero-Isaiah, a prophet of the school of Isaiah, foresees the totally new event in the Servant of Yahweh who alone is the one not to be astounded that "God loves me, a sinner". He is "one-of-us", but not a sinner. In him God loves all sinners. Freely he bears the burden of us all and leads us to the awesome truth that, in him and through him, God shows us so great a love. "Ours were the sufferings he bore, ours the sorrows he carried. But we thought of him as someone punished by God, struck by God, brought low. Yet he was pierced through our faults, crushed for our sins. On him lies the atonement that brings peace, and through his wounds we are healed" (Is 53: 4–5).

Seeing the pierced heart of Jesus, all quarrels about who among us might be the greater sinner — or saint — are senseless. We can only say all together in awed amazement: "So much are we sinners (am I a sinner) loved by God and his faithful Son and Servant!" From this follows the "law of Christ" that we should all willingly bear each other's burdens (Gal 6: 2).

* * *

Compassionate heart of Jesus, have mercy on me. I say it now, and give me the grace to say it always. Even before I had offended you, I was not entitled to receive such great signs of your graciousness, O my Saviour! You have created me, you have granted me so much light, all without any merit on my part. But after having offended you I had not only no merit whatsoever but deserved to be abandoned for hell. It is only because of your compassionate love that you waited and kept me in life while I lived in disgrace. Your compassionate kindness enlightened me and invited me to reconciliation, and inspired in me contrition for my sins and desire to love you.

And now, by your mercy, I hope to live in your grace. My Jesus, never stop showing me your favour. The mercy I ask is that you grant me light and strength never again to be thankless. I surely do not pretend that you are obliged to forgive me when I again turn away from you; this would be nothing less than presumption and resistance to your compassionate love. And for what reason would I ever again refuse your friendship? This must never happen! Dear Jesus, my love belongs forever to you. And this is the mercy I hope for and humbly ask: let me never be separated from you!

(Prayer of St Alphonsus)

5

"Late did I come to love you"

"Yahweh says this: They have found pardon in the wilderness, those who have survived the sword. Israel is marching to his rest. Yahweh has appeared to him from afar: I have loved you with an everlasting love, so I am constant in my affection to you. . . . For I am a father to Israel, and Ephraim is my first-born son. . . . He who has scattered Israel gathers him, he guards him as a shepherd guards his flock" (Jer 31:2–10).

"Show forbearance and a consistently gentle disposition towards all men. For at one time we ourselves in our folly and obstinacy were all astray. We were slaves of passions and pleasures of every kind. Our days were passed in malice and envy; we were odious ourselves and we hated one another. But when the kindness and generosity of God our Saviour dawned upon the world, then, not for any good deeds of our own, but because he was merciful, he saved us through the water of rebirth and the renewing power of the Holy Spirit" (Tit 3:2–5).

EVEN today St Augustine's word, "Late did I come to love you", speaks to the hearts of many people, for they have gone through a similar experience. It expresses both deep regret for so many lost years and grateful praise for the infinite forbearance and faithfulness of God.

Further, the personal experience joins in the solidary grief of the people of God, the Church, that so many of its members and officials, in their individual and collective practices, have for a long time resisted God's grace and his appeal for total conversion and renewal. But the decisive aspect is that this sorrow, as in the "Confessions of St Augustine", inspires praise of God for his patience and for the final victory of his love.

We praise him, too, for the gift of so many saints, known

and unknown to us, who finally came to a perfect love of God. When St Teresa of Avila had come to a unique experience of God's love and of being overwhelmed by it, she could only wonder in deep humility how she could have lived a superficial life for so many years despite all the opportunities for the better choice. If we imprison ourselves in trifles or lack the firm purpose and clear decision to make our hearts totally free for the Lord, we not only deprive ourselves of the joy of the Lord, the inner peace and the blissful experience of God's love for us, but we also impoverish the whole Church, indeed the life of the world.

In most cases it is not a matter of enslavement to devastating passions, as was the case with the young Augustine; rather, it is the lack of a firm decision to allow Christ to take hold of our whole being: our heart, our mind and our will. St Alphonsus compares the attitude of some people to an eagle who allows itself to be tied by a thin thread instead of breaking it and taking flight into the heights.

But the amazing truth is that, in spite of our shallowness, the Lord does not abandon us. He continues to "court" us for an undivided love, time and again touching our hearts, giving us a foretaste of the bliss that could be ours if only we would allow his love to conquer us fully.

It would be unconscientious presumption to think that we have a certain right to our Lord's patience because we have shown occasional moments of fervour and have tried to avoid at least mortal sins and scandal. This, in the midst of a superficiality that seduces us to give only second place to the love of God, surely does not entitle us to any kind of self-exaltation. In his book *Novena to the Sacred Heart* St Alphonsus offers a special meditation entitled "The grateful heart of Jesus" in which he praises the kindness of Jesus who appreciates even our small steps towards full conversion and all small efforts to please him. If Jesus treats us so kindly and patiently, it is all to the glory of the Father with no merit on our part. We should be very much aware of this as an added motive for gratitude and generosity.

A deep sorrow for having wasted so many precious years and so many unrepeatable opportunities to please God by serving the cause of his kingdom is, in itself, a sign that God is gracious and continues to draw us to his heart. This sorrow, expressed in frequent prayer of thanksgiving, praise and humble petition for a renewed heart, opens us to the superabundant grace that God has prepared for us.

The firm decision to seek and to do at all times and in all events what pleases God must take deep roots in our heart, in our memory and our will, in our conscious and subconscious life. Our motives and intentions have to be purified and confirmed in the fire of the love of Jesus. No more time must be wasted.

* * *

Late did I come to love you, O eternal and ever new beauty; late, indeed, did I come to love you. You were within me but I was outside looking for you like a bold intruder in your beautiful world. You were with me but I was not with you. You called me, you cried in a loud voice and finally broke my deafness. You bathed me in your light, you wrapped me in your splendour, and drove away my blindness. You gave out a delightful fragrance, and I breathed it in and was longing for you. I have tasted and am hungry and thirsty for you. You have touched me, and I burn to know your peace.

If I cling to you with all my heart, then I do not mind pain and toil. My life, if it is full of you, is thoroughly alive.

But I, whom you lift up, am still a burden to myself, for I am not totally full of you. My joys are mixed with tears, my smile with sadness. And still I am not sure to which side victory is inclining.

Look on me, O Lord, have mercy on me! There is still war between my evil afflictions and my good joys, and still I am not sure where victory lies. Lord, have mercy; look on my wounds. I do not try to conceal them. You are the physician, I am the patient. You are merciful, I am miserable.

All my hope is in your great mercy. Grant me what you command and command what you will. O Love that ever glows and is never extinguished, O divine Love, my God, inflame me!

(Prayer of St Augustine, *Confessions*, X)

6

We are dear to Jesus, like his mother, if . . .

> "Jesus was still speaking to the crowd when his mother and brothers appeared; they stood outside, wanting to speak to him. Someone said, 'Your mother and your brothers are outside; they want to speak with you'. Jesus turned to the man who brought the message, and said, 'Who is my mother? Who are my brothers?' And pointing to the disciples, he said, 'Here are my mother and my brothers. Whoever does the will of my heavenly Father is my brother, my sister, my mother' " (Mt 12:46–50).

THE heart of Jesus, filled with love for us, is particularly near to his mother. It was formed in her virginal womb, and there it began to beat in perfect consonance with her heart. The tender love of the most loving mother on earth gave Jesus his first human experience of affection and dedication.

No doubt, since the first awakening of Jesus' consciousness, the unforgettable tenderness of his mother's love was written in his heart. He would have understood well the prophet's word: "Can a woman forget the infant at her breast, or a loving mother the child of her womb? Yet even if these forget, I will never forget you" (Is 49:15).

Jesus' great mission was to reveal to us the love of God, our Father, through our understanding of human fatherly and motherly love and beyond it. In this mission, his mother had a privileged role, first by communicating to Jesus the most tender and faithful motherly love, and then by joining him in the courageous and generous revelation of his love, unto the moment when she stood under his cross and saw him die.

A genuine devotion to the Sacred Heart of Jesus naturally includes devotion to the loving Heart of Mary, his mother and our mother. We are grateful to her for the love she gave to

Jesus, and we praise her for the love she received from him. She fulfilled for humanity the role as the new Eve, side-by-side with her Son.

In and through all of her life, Mary is the "Magnificat", an everlasting praise of God, the all-merciful: "His mercy is from generation to generation" (Lk 1:50). John Paul II wrote in his encyclical *Dives in Misericordia*: "No one has taken this mystery to heart as Mary has: the truly divine dimension of redemption wrought on Golgotha through the death of the Son of God, together with the sacrifice of the heart of Mary in her definitive 'fiat' " (no. 9).

We do not want to overstress the psychic ties between Jesus and his mother. Real as they were, they are not the decisive fact. Jesus had to detach himself from Nazareth, from his relatives and even from his mother, for the sake of the "new family of God", of which he is the origin, and for total dedication to the good news of the coming kingdom. This detachment is already prefigured by the decision of the twelve-year-old Jesus to remain in the Temple while Mary and Joseph and the other pilgrims return to their homes.

However, the detachment goes hand-in-hand with a new and stronger bond between the Son and his mother who, better than anyone else, hears the good news, keeps it in her heart, ponders over it and puts it into practice. She is Jesus' first disciple and follows him unto the end on Calvary.

When the humble, prophetic woman praises Jesus' mother, saying, "Happy the womb that carried you and the breast that suckled you", Jesus turns his listeners' attention to what best distinguishes Mary and his new family: "Rather, happy are those who hear the word of God and keep it" (Lk 11:27–28). The same gospel leaves no doubt that Mary is the outstanding model of this practice (cf. Lk 2:19; 2:51).

By continuing to preach the good news while his mother and brothers waited outside, Jesus taught us that in the "new family of God" spiritual relationships are more decisive than physical ones. But again he points implicitly to the outstanding model of these spiritual relationships: "Anyone who does the will of my Father in heaven is my brother, my sister, my mother" (Mt 12:50).

Mary is uniquely privileged in the Father's design for the

redemption and election of all, and unique also is the love that Jesus shows to his mother. With her he rejoices in the praise of the heavenly Father and from her he learned in his childhood the songs of praise of Israel, particularly the songs of the Servant of Yahweh which he made the programme of his life. He knows that his mother is "full of grace". In her the good news yields the richest and most precious harvest; she is the total "yes" to the will of God.

Hanging on the cross, Jesus turned to the "woman" foretold in Genesis whose offspring was to crush the head of the serpent (cf. Gen 3:15), and entrusted to her the beloved disciple — representing all of us — while also entrusting the mother to his disciple. "And from that moment the disciple took her into his home" (Jn 19:27). We, too, take her into our home, into our heart, if we take the word of God into our heart and keep it, even if, like Mary, we have to stand in the shadow of the cross.

* * *

Oh my Saviour, I praise you for the tender and faithful love that filled your heart unto its last beat on the cross. You have done so much to draw us all to you! Indeed, my heart is filled with joy when I remember that you compare your love for us poor sinners to your love for your holy mother.

You assure us that we can be as near to your heart as she is if, with her, we join you in loving and doing the will of our heavenly Father. It is a mighty challenge and a powerful incentive for us to follow you in your total surrender to the loving will of the Father, even unto death. By this comforting and demanding word you show us how wholly you were consecrated to the Father, so that we, too, with Mary your mother, might be consecrated in truth. What more could you have done to spur us on to receive your word with grateful and loving hearts and to put it into practice!

But if I examine closely the condition under which I may come as close to your heart as your mother, then my mediocrity and superficiality makes me angry with myself. What a fool I must be to jeopardize such a promise! Lord, forgive me; give me strength to renounce everything that hinders me on the road to this bliss. Help me always to hear your word and keep it — like your mother!

7

Jesus honours us as a gift of the Father

> "The glory which thou gavest me I have given to them, that they may be one, as we are one; I in them and thou in me, may they be perfectly one. Then the world will learn that thou didst send me, that thou didst love them as thou didst me. Father, I desire that these men, who are thy gift to me, may be with me where I am, so that they may look upon my glory, which thou hast given me because thou didst love me before the world began. I made thy name known to them, and will make it known, so that the love thou hast for me may be in them, and I may be in them" (Jn 17:22–26).

GOD speaks to the heart of the chosen people in many startling images about his love for them. He loves Israel more than a father loves his child. His love is more tender than that of all mothers. His love is pictured in the contexture of the love between bridegroom and bride. No vine-dresser takes care of his vines as he takes care of his people. But all this good news is only a prelude to the full revelation of his love in Jesus Christ.

In the gospel Jesus surprises us with totally unexpected sayings, such as: "Whoever does the will of my heavenly Father is my brother, my sister, my mother" (Mt 12:50). He allows us and invites us to call his Father "our Father". His unique relationship with the Father as the only-begotten, eternal Son does not allow him to say that we are dear to him in the same way as his Father; yet what he tells us about his disciples' share in that relationship surpasses anything that men might imagine. Here we are faced with messages from Jesus which transform our heart, our whole life, and fill us with abiding joy if we receive them in faith.

Probably the most heart-moving texts are found in Jesus' farewell prayer particularly in the words: "that thou didst love them as thou didst me" (Jn 17:23), and climaxing in the concluding words: "that the love thou hast for me may be in them, and I may be in them" (Jn 17:26). The Father has not only revealed his love in the loving heart of Jesus and given us Jesus as model, but has made, as it were, the loving disciples of Christ, the true believers, a part of the love between the Father and Jesus.

In another heart-stirring message Jesus says: "As the Father has loved me, so I have loved you" (Jn 15:9). The heart of Jesus, glowing with love for us, is here the "open port" through which he introduces us into the life of the triune God. We can respond only by adoring this mystery of God's astonishing self-revelation.

If, as believers and loving disciples of Jesus, we join him in his "Abba, Father", it is the Holy Spirit who then prays in us and who enables us to say it so truthfully that it will mark all of our life and all of our relationships (cf. Rom 8:15; Gal 4:6). "Because God's love has flooded our inmost heart through the Holy Spirit he has given us" (Rom 5:5).

In his high-priestly prayer Jesus expresses four times the blissful message that he considers his disciples as a special gift of the Father and that therefore they are dear to his heart. "I pray for them . . . for those whom thou hast given me; because they belong to thee. All that is mine is thine, and what is thine is mine, and through them has my glory shone" (Jn 17:9–10). Jesus knows himself as being sent for us (cf. Jn 17:3–25). It follows that Jesus and those who cling to him in faith are a gift of the Father for each other in an ineffable mutuality. What greater incentive could there ever be to love Jesus, to love with him the Father, and to love with the Father and Jesus all of God's children?

In the name of Jesus, whom the Father has given us, we can pray with unlimited trust. But this name leads us to pray above all for grateful love for him and the Father. Time and again and with ever increasing awe and amazement we will meditate on the truth that, as believers, we can love the heavenly Father with the love of Jesus and, in return, love Jesus with the love of the Father. And immersed in the life of the Father, the Son and the Holy Spirit, we can love each other and accept and honour each other as gift from the Father.

This, then, is our life's programme offered us by Jesus when, speaking "from heart to heart" with the Father, he takes us, his disciples, most wonderfully into this dialogue. In this exchange of love we join with the heart of Jesus, glowing with love for his Father and his brothers and sisters and ready to manifest his love and trust even on the cross. With him we entrust ourselves to the Father and his loving will, though we might not yet understand it in all its dimensions.

Being thus at home with Jesus and the Father in the abiding love of the Spirit, we begin to grasp the beauty of our mission: "As the Father has loved me, so I have loved you. Dwell in my love. . . Love one another as I have loved you" (Jn 15 : 9–12).

* * *

Our dear Saviour, when you spoke from heart to heart with your heavenly Father you made your disciples — indeed, all of us believers — an intimate part of this exchange of love and trust. I would never dare to feel included if your disciples had been immaculate and blameless. You chose them when they were still unlike you. You foreknew their failure when the time of your ordeal would come, yet you took them wholly into that wonderful exchange with the Father. And so even I, a sinner, can dare to think that I, too, was included. O wonder of wonders!

We praise you, Father, Lord of heaven and earth, for having revealed in Jesus your great love for us together with your love for your only Son. Through his loving heart you have shown us the way to your heart's inmost mystery of love. He whom you have sent tells us: "He who loves me will be loved by my Father; and I will love him and disclose myself to him. . . Anyone who loves me will heed what I say; then the Father will love him, and we will come to him and make our dwelling with him" (Jn 14 : 21–23). This assurance makes me forget all my own wishes. All else pales before this blissful light, and at the same time all that is good, true and beautiful shines forth in your light. Everything is your gift, and all your gifts call us to love you.

Your supreme and all-encompassing gift to us is Jesus, in whom the fullness of the godhead dwells, in whom and through whom you share with us your own love. This unsurpassable gift assures us that if we pray with faith, you will give us the second gift: a new heart which will be able to love you and Jesus worthily, a heart filled with your Spirit and overflowing with generosity and kindness for all of your children. Now and always I shall beg you: grant us this love, this new heart. Let us now and forever be at home in the heart of Jesus, so that we may love you with his love.

8

Only love counts

> "If I speak in tongues of men or of angels, but if I am without love, I am a sounding gong or a clanging cymbal. I may have the gift of prophecy, and know every hidden truth; I may have faith enough to move mountains; but if I have no love, I am nothing. I may dole out all I possess, or even give my body to be burnt, but if I have no love, I am none the better" (1 Cor 13 : 1–3).

GOD is love and all his works and words are the overflow and revelation of his love. The supreme manifestation of his love for us sinful people is that he sent us his only Son who, in loving obedience to the mandate of his Father, gave himself up totally for us. Should we investigate all God's work but be unmindful of his love, we would completely miss the mark. Indeed, we would miss God himself. Not only would the deepest meaning and beauty remain concealed from us but without the code of love we could not rightly decipher God's loving will regarding his various works and gifts.

Surely, God requests good deeds from us, but not as our own achievement to boast about, not as something done without love. What matters is love itself, offered with all our heart and all our vigour, as response to God's love for us. What really counts is the love of people who are so imbued with his love that its fruits arise from their innermost being. Only thus are we "in the truth", a created image of the eternal Word that breathes love, the Holy Spirit, the "Spirit of truth". By its very nature such love is fruitful, having its deep roots in Jesus' love of which he makes us sharers.

This is the marvellous vision given us by John's gospel. "He who dwells in me, as I dwell in him, bears much fruit; for apart from me you can do nothing. . . If you dwell in me, and my words dwell in you, ask what you will and you shall have it.

This is my Father's glory, that you may bear fruit in plenty and so be my disciples" (Jn 15 : 5–8).

Jesus wants us to be fully aware that the initiative of this loving union and sharing is his own: "You did not choose me: I have chosen you. I appointed you to go on and bear fruit, fruit that shall last; so that the Father may give you all that you ask in my name. This then is my commandment to you: love one another" (Jn 15 : 16–17).

Here we touch one of the essential points of the devotion to the Sacred Heart. If, lovingly, we make our abiding home in the heart of Jesus and entrust ourselves wholly to him, we discover that we can love with heart and hands, with memory and intellect, with affections and firm purpose. We can trustfully embrace our mission. By the love that flows from the heart of Jesus, our intellect becomes lucid, sensitive, alert. The heart inflamed and seized by Christ's love forges the will for what is good.

This was already the peak of the Old Testament revelation. God, the revealer and redeemer, speaks to the hearts of his people: "And now, Israel, what does Yahweh your God ask of you? Only this: to fear Yahweh, your God, to follow all his ways, to love him, to serve Yahweh, your God, with all your heart and all your soul" (Deut 10 : 12).

Bringing the Old Testament prophecies to fulfilment, Jesus not only tells us that this all-encompassing commandment can be fulfilled by the redeemed who trust in his grace, he also takes us by the hand and introduces us into the beauty of his love and of a life totally dedicated to this love.

The three great steps for those devoted to the Heart of Jesus are: to learn how to love Jesus and the Father in heaven; to learn what it means to love, with Jesus and "in Jesus", our neighbour and all those loved by him; and last but not least, to pray unceasingly for the gift of the Spirit who breathes love into our hearts and grants us the discernment to distinguish between redeemed love and its counterfeits.

In this learning process it is important to see clearly how the love-response embraces and includes all virtues and all divine commandments, and that these are, just as love itself is, gracious gifts of God. Here we touch a central task of christian education and moral theology.

That love alone counts has been a part of our best Catholic

tradition, especially in view of the evangelical counsels and the religious vows.

Virginity and celibacy for the sake of God's kingdom draw their strength and direction from one's being seized by God's love. They make sense only to those whose hearts are filled with the love of Jesus. Married people, as well as those who renounce marriage for God's kingdom, must give careful attention to loving God in himself in response to his infinite love, and never to "use God" for their own purposes. Our love of neighbour, too, is chaste in the most profound meaning of the word if it flows from the depths of our heart, a love that will never be tempted to instrumentalize him.

Celibacy as charism shines with special brilliance when the disciples of Christ have the inner strength to love and serve the unloved, the despised, those not yet able to respond with love in return; and to love them with that love which they learn from Jesus and for which they pray with faith to him who is the source of such a love.

Evangelical poverty has at least three essential dimensions. The precondition for experiencing poverty as beatitude is to free our heart, mind and will from everything that hinders us from a truly wholehearted love of the Lord. It is a matter of opening space for his love, indeed, all the space. Further, the charism of poverty implies that the believer experiences the grace and beatitude of a "life in Christ" to such an extent that these very riches allow him or her to renounce many things by which others are kept in slavery. An inner freedom makes it acceptable and even desirable to renounce everything that might conceal the joy of faith and peace or diminish our witness to the plentiful riches found in this life in Christ. The third dimension of this charism is that from this very experience and inner change comes the supreme art of offering to our neighbour not only things and services but the much greater gift of our affection, genuine love and affirmative respect.

How poor are those children whose parents give them thousands of things but are unable or unwilling to give themselves, their hearts' love, their affirmation and time! A happy father of seven told me this story: After the Christmas holidays there was a family meeting at his house. The children of the other families began to boast about the many expensive gifts they had received.

After a moment's silence, a surprising comment came from his ten-year-old Elisabeth. To these children, each of whom was an "only" child, she retorted: "And we have Joseph, John, Francis, Antonia, Agatha, Catherine; and whom do you have?" It was a revelation from a child's heart and lips about what is true wealth.

Christian obedience, as well as celibacy and evangelical poverty, receives its meaning and purpose from the freedom to love, to care, to affirm one's neighbour. The exercise of authority and attention to the common good becomes the response to the way Christ was obedient and at the same time an embodiment of prophetic freedom.

In this sense St Ignatius of Loyola gives meaning to his motto, "Everything for the greater glory of God", through loving conformation with Christ. "When it is a matter of discerning what equally might be for the greater glory of God, I look at Christ and how I can follow him most intimately and become more like him. Therefore I love and prefer poverty with Christ rather than riches. I prefer to be insulted with Christ rather than to be honoured. I prefer to be considered an insignificant man and a fool for Christ's sake rather than to be praised as wise and clever in this world". Such a choice makes sense only to loving hearts.

* * *

Lord Jesus Christ, full of love and worthy of all love, you are the Father's greatest gift to us. You not only offer us countless precious gifts; you give us yourself with all your love. You open for us the treasures of your loving heart, and it is this heart's love that gives to all your gifts an infinite value. Through them you speak to our hearts.

What thanks can I offer you, Lord Jesus, except my love in return with all my heart? And, as another wonderful gift, you let me know that you accept it for no other reason than that of your own love for me, which is the origin of my response.

But how could I have dared, during so many years, to offer you no more than a superficial, divided and inconsistent love? A thousand times I have deserved to hear you say that you refuse to accept such a mixture of good and poor motives. It is only your merciful love that moved you to look graciously on my yearning to purify my affections and find a better way of loving you. For this very purpose you have allowed suffering and constraints to afflict me; you have granted me insight and strength to learn in the school of suffering. You are showing me the road to bring all this home into my thanksgiving. Yes, Lord, I know that in all things you work tenderly to purify my heart and to conquer it for your blissful friendship.

Lord, I begin to understand that only love can be the proper response, a love that comes from you and leads to you. Now and unto the last breath of my life, unto the last heart-beat, I shall not pray for anything more than the grace to love you with all my heart, all my soul, all my strength. Increase this yearning so that I may become ready to receive this greatest gift.

9

The greatest love is not loved in return

> "Let me sing to my friend
> the song of his love for his vineyard.
> My friend had a vineyard on a fertile hillside.
> He dug the soil, cleared it of stones,
> and planted choice vines in it.
> In the middle of it he built a tower,
> he dug a press there too.
> He expected it to yield grapes,
> but sour grapes were all that it gave.
> And now, inhabitants of Jerusalem and men of Judah,
> I ask you to judge between me and my vineyard.
> What could I have done for my vineyard that I have not done? . . .
>
> Yes, the vineyard of the Lord of hosts is the house of Israel
> and the people of Judah that chosen plant" (Is 45 : 1–7).

THE Old Testament prophets rightly saw the refusal of a great part of Israel to love God faithfully as a shocking and frightening event. God himself complains, through the prophets, about this thanklessness of hardened hearts. He asks his chosen people: "What more could I have done for you?"

This question becomes even more heart-rending when those who are faced with the heart of Jesus opened for us and his blood shed for us have refused their love to God who has done wondrous things to reveal his love and to touch our hearts. Contemplating, on the one hand, the overflowing love of the heart of Jesus and, on the other, the dire reality, many saints have cried out in pain: "The greatest love is not loved!"

It is alarming to see the prophecy fulfilled that "love in most men will grow cold" (Mt 24 : 12), even in many parts of christianity. No wonder that men's love for one another grows cold when they do not care to respond even to God's own love for us. They cut themselves off from the source of all love.

How terribly the heart of Jesus must have been afflicted, seeing how quickly the ardour of many in the crowd, who had listened to him and had experienced his healing love and power, had grown cold! He saw even his closest disciples abandon him. All this presaged for Jesus what would happen throughout history.

The anguished laments, which the liturgy ascribes to Jesus, recur again and again in the history of the devotion to the Sacred Heart. "I hoped for sympathy, but in vain, I found no one to console me" (Ps 69:20). This aspect is a striking dimension in the religious experience of St Margaret Mary Alacoque. The hearts of believers are deeply moved when on Good Friday they hear: "My people, what have I done to you? Did I ever grieve you? Answer me!"

If we truly believe and have sensitive hearts, we cannot but be deeply troubled by this devastating lovelessness that assails the heart of Jesus, pierced for us first by the soldier's lance and pierced again in every generation by the cold steel of the hearts of men.

Jesus' pain is, above all, for the offence and insult given to his heavenly Father by this crying injustice of men's refusal to love him despite the supreme revelation of his love for them. He sees also the disastrous consequences of this mindless ingratitude, of man's locking his heart to saving love and poisoning his environment by his heartless "no". It is, indeed, the extreme act of self-destruction, of vandalism directed against the most noble potentialities of the human being, who is still called to find his or her perfection and joy in thankful response to God's love. How can Jesus not be afflicted by this senseless vandalism, this turning against one's milieu, when thankful love would have created a new person and a new environment radiating peace?

Whoever refuses God his love becomes, by this very injustice, pregnant with injustice against fellowmen, a source of lovelessness, frustration, injustice, deception. He becomes a slave and makes others slaves of the "sin of the world", of solidarity in evil. If I sin, it is always a lack of love for God which decreases my capacity to love him, my neighbour and myself with a true love. I become a partial cause of a growing coldness of heart in the world. My sin strikes back not only against me but also against the common good. One who refuses God's love is choosing, instead, the heavy chains of collective sinfulness in all its forms.

This reflection is central to the devotion to the Sacred Heart when it comes from a heart touched by the all-embracing love of Jesus. If our reflection is authentic, it will lead to a deep and liberating sorrow and to a burning desire to offer Jesus and the Father the satisfaction of true love. It will lead also to an effective compassion with all people who are lukewarm and to a desire to help them to strive to love God with all their heart.

John, the beloved disciple, standing by the cross, saw the terrible and yet so significant event when the soldier pierced the heart of Jesus with his lance. Telling of this he quotes the Scripture which is now fulfilled, expecting us to be mindful of it: "They shall look on him whom they have pierced" (Jn 19:37). The first part turns our attention, our memory, our eyes and heart to this heart pierced for us. The second part expects us to remember that our sins were there, in the terrible game of wounding the heart of Jesus. For us, as loving, grateful and repentant believers, this meditation can produce both a deep sorrow for our sins, grief for all human sins and, at the same time, can inflame our hearts with a fervent and faithful love. The Old Testament text quoted by John expresses best the fruits of such a loving contemplation: "Over the house of David and the citizens of Jerusalem I will pour out a spirit of kindness and prayer. They will look on him whom they have pierced" (Zech 12:10).

The lives of many saints tell us how the shock of seeing such a meagre response to the boundless love of God, coupled with the grateful remembrance of the heart of Jesus, pierced by us and for us, can produce a profound change of heart, mind and will, and of our fundamental relationships, indeed, of our whole life.

* * *

Loving heart of Jesus, you chose poverty on earth so that nothing could conceal the wealth of the love which you offer us. Freely you espouse all the turmoil, all the fatigue and risks of a homeless preacher to proclaim everywhere that the kingdom of love is at hand. You gathered disciples around you to let them feel the warmth of your friendship, the tenderness of your healing and redeeming love.

Not only with words did you teach us that "there is no greater love than this, that a man should lay down his life for his friends" (Jn 15 : 13). With the supreme purpose of revealing the height and depth, the length and breadth of your love and that of the Father, you have stretched out your arms for us on the cross. You have allowed the lance to pierce your heart and have given for us the last drop of your most precious blood. Surely, if anyone does not love you and your heavenly Father there is no excuse.

Lord Jesus, it grieves me to know that so many people do not care at all for your love and prefer to remain slaves of a devastating self-love and individual and collective egotism. Even more painful is the thought that many of those who had begun to rejoice in your love have broken their commitment to you, have turned to poisoned cisterns, refusing you, the source of living water.

It is shocking that even priests and religious have abandoned their first love and behave as if they had never known you. But the most piercing pain for me is to realize that I, too, have withheld part of my love while making senseless investments of it. Faced with the fact that the love of many is growing cold, I beg you: Inflame my heart wholly with your love and send me to win over the hearts of many for your love.

10

Heart of Jesus, transform our hearts

> "I kneel in prayer to the Father, from whom every family in heaven and on earth takes its name, that out of the treasures of his glory he may grant you strength and power through his Spirit in your inner being, that through faith Christ may dwell in your hearts in love. With deep roots and firm foundations, may you be strong to grasp, with all God's people, what is the breadth and length and height and depth of the love of Christ, and to know it, though it is beyond knowledge. So may you attain to fullness of being, the fullness of God himself" (Eph 3 : 14–19).

MARK synthesizes the preaching of Jesus in these words: "The time has come; the kingdom of God is upon you; repent, and believe the Gospel" (Mk 1 : 15). The Greek word which we translate as either "repent" or "be converted" is *metanoeite*. It means a whole new way of thinking, feeling, longing: a new heart. We could translate it as "Be renewed in your heart". The good news is that now the promised time has come when God himself, by the power of the Spirit, will create in us a new heart. "I shall bring you home. I shall pour clean water over you and you will be cleansed; I shall cleanse you from all your defilements and all your idols. I shall give you a new heart, and put a new spirit in you; I shall remove the heart of stone from you and give you a sensitive heart instead. I shall put my spirit in you" (Ezek 36 : 24–26; cf. Jer 31 : 33).

This wonderful transformation cannot happen through a mere imperative of new laws and structures in the outer world. It happens through faith, by allowing the good news to take hold of us, entrusting ourselves totally to God who, in Jesus, opens the treasures of his love for us. In this way God writes his grace and law into our hearts (Jer 31 : 33). Eye to eye and heart to heart with Jesus, we become new people. We think, feel, yearn and love differently. We see God through the eyes of thankful love. There is a knowledge of the *good*, of what is good, true and beautiful, accessible only to a heart renewed in love.

The great mystics who venerated the Sacred Heart communicate this truth in various moving images. Cardinal Newman, for instance, is inspired by the image of St John resting on Jesus' heart. He speaks of the disciple's longing for a perfect love of Jesus, "until heart in heart reposes", "heart speaks to heart". Others speak of the "arrow of love" coming from Jesus' heart and piercing our heart. It is a flame of love that wounds and at the same time heals the heart. Some speak of an "exchange of hearts" offered by Jesus himself to those who yearn for his love.

St Augustine calls Jesus the "joy of the pure heart" in the same sense that Jesus calls "blessed" those whose hearts are pure: "they shall see God" (Mt 5 : 8). Touched and purified they now see with "eyes of love". For St Paul this means that "through faith" Jesus "dwells in our hearts in love" (Eph 3 : 17). Justification and sanctification are the work of grace through faith bearing fruit in love, a new way of knowing God "with the heart", configured to the heart of Jesus, "to be without blemish in his sight and full of love" (Eph 1 : 4).

In Holy Scripture the word "heart" frequently means a conscience sensitive to God's calling and to everything that is good, a conscience guided and illumined by love. For the Christian this means knowing Jesus lovingly and considering everything in the sight of God. It implies a reciprocity of consciences in a saving solidarity by those whose hearts have been won by the love of the Redeemer. With the new heart comes also a new horizon of discernment. We think as members of God's family.

All this powerful attraction and transformation is grace, insertion into Christ's life. Jesus tells us: "Nobody comes to me unless he is drawn by the Father who sent me" (Jn 6 : 44). "No one knows who the Son is but the Father, nor who the Father is but the Son, and those to whom the Son may choose to reveal him" (Lk 10 : 22).

Entering into the realm of truth and love through the gate of Jesus' heart, being at home in this loving heart, reposing beside Jesus, the disciple has a new kind of conscience. Everything appears in a new light and has new beauty. Every virtue and every law of God receives its proper place in the whole picture and becomes attractive. One's conscience thus becomes alert for the signs of the times, for what the present hour offers, and for the many opportunities to give witness to Christ and his kingdom.

This change of heart and conscience can be seen in the light of Jesus' word: "Come to me all whose work is hard, whose load is heavy; and I will give you relief. Bend your necks to my yoke, and learn from me; for I am gentle and humble-hearted; and your souls will find relief. For my yoke is good to bear, my load is light" (Mt 11:28–30).

The storm of our passions, slavish fear and anguish cease when we repose near the heart of Jesus. We feel new strength, new joy in doing God's will, knowing it not as a law imposed but as an invitation to live as beloved and loving children, as intimate friends. Thus also the decisions of our conscience become more trustful, creative and generous.

In this context of the biblical meaning of "heart" we may also say that reposing in Jesus' heart affects even our unconscious life, our subconscious. Not even the best psychotherapists can liberate our conscious and subconscious psychic life as surely as does a new heart-to-heart relationship with Jesus. Rapt in the love of Jesus, a grateful memory opens new avenues for grasping present opportunities, for reshaping past tendencies, and opens new doors for future hope and creativity.

For those who live closest to the heart of Jesus, the transformation of conscience will lead not only to some courageous decisions, after a hard fight against the "old Adam" in us, but also to an ever more ready response to our neighbour's needs, and in a way that radiates joy and peace.

Jesus instructs us: "What comes out of the mouth has its origins in the heart" (Mt 15:18), and "The words that the mouth utters come from the heart" (Mt 12:34). We also remember the word: "Where your treasure is, there will your heart be also" (Mt 6:21). The "formation of conscience" by laws and precepts, and even by criteria for discernment, is one thing; quite another and much farther-reaching and fruitful is the formation of depth-conscience in a heart-to-heart friendship with Jesus.

Those who in all things seek first the kingdom of God, whose hearts beat with the heart of Jesus in a love that surpasses all concepts, are best prepared for seeking and finding what is good, truthful and beautiful. Drawn by the love of Christ, the depth-conscience, like a magnetic needle, will point to a clear orientation of life.

The insights of depth-psychology about the great importance of our unconscious and subconscious forces are far from being a denial of freedom. Quite the contrary! If we learn to heal our memory, to fill it with thankfulness and loving attention, if we allow Jesus to conquer our hearts for his love and for loving our neighbour with him, our "souls will find relief"; we will come to a truly "hearty" health and a new freedom for trust and love.

* * *

O my dear Lord, I need thee to teach me day by day according to each day's opportunities and needs. I need thee to give me a true divine instinct about revealed matters. Give me the gift of discriminating between true and false in all discourse of mind. And for that end, give me that purity of conscience which alone can receive, which alone can improve thy inspirations.

My ears are dull, so that I cannot hear thy voice. My eyes are dim, so that I cannot see thy tokens. Thou alone canst quicken my hearing, and purge my sight, and cleanse and renew my heart.

Teach me, like Mary, to sit at thy feet, and hear thy word. Give me true wisdom which seeks thy will by prayer and meditation, by direct intercourse with thee more than by reading and reasoning.

I believe, O my Saviour, that thou lovest me better than I love myself. I know thou wilt do thy part towards me, as I, through thy grace, desire to do my part towards thee. I know well thou never canst forsake those who seek thee, or canst disappoint those who trust thee.

Keep me ever from being afraid of thine eye, from the inward consciousness that I am not honestly trying to please thee.

Teach me to love thee more, and then I shall be at peace, without any fear of thee at all.

And at the place thou hast assigned me, I shall be a messenger of thy peace.

(Prayer of Cardinal John Henry Newman)

11

Only love can atone

> "Fortitude you have, you have borne up in my cause and never flagged. But I have this against you: you have lost your early love. Think from what height you have fallen; repent and do as once you did" (Rev 2:3–5).

> "These are the words of the Son of God, whose eyes flame like fire and whose feet gleam like burnished brass: I know all your ways, your love and faithfulness, your good service and fortitude; and of late you have done even better than at first" (Rev 2:18–19).

THE reader has now gone with me a long way. I hope it is now the right moment to speak of atonement, which in the official devotion to the Sacred Heart plays an important role. This dimension seems to be inaccessible for many. There are some who require dire mortifications, hard works of reparation, without seeing the foundations and purpose of atonement. Others reject the devotion immediately because of such or other misinterpretations.

At the beginning of their conversion many saints, including Blessed Henry Suso, the great promoter of the devotion to the Sacred Heart, imposed on themselves cruel chastisements, even to the detriment of health; but at a certain point the Lord gave them the insight that he does not want this kind of atonement. Henry Suso was taught to atone with heartfelt love, unlimited trust and total conformity to the loving will of God. In a similar way St Margaret Mary Alacoque came to the same understanding. While jansenistic nuns requested hard external penances, the humble nun of Pary-le-Monial transmitted the message of the Sacred Heart that love alone counts for atonement. From deep sorrow for one's own sins and for the grievous lack of love offered to God who is love arose an insatiable desire to atone with a pure and fervent love for Jesus, and thus united with Jesus "unto death" to offer satisfaction to the Father.

The first question about atonement, therefore, cannot be what kind of suffering should we inflict upon ourselves. We should not at all afflict ourselves with useless suffering. Rather, the question is how to achieve that great love which atones for our earlier lack of love and for the refusal of love by which so many people offend God. We must yearn for this love, pray for it, since it is an undeserved gift of God, and then accept all the sacrifices required to express our love in the service of our brothers and sisters.

St Augustine describes the history of salvation and, indeed, the history of the world as a relentless battle between two kinds of love: pure, strong and grateful love of God which engenders a redeemed and redeeming love of neighbour, and a perverted self-love.

The first step in atoning-love is to strive faithfully towards the purification of our love *at any cost*. As Pius XI explained, the veneration of the Sacred Heart implies "a repentant love" and a "love attentive to satisfaction". He exemplified this especially by calling for a simple style of life and by sacrifices which are indispensable if we are to manifest an effective love for those in need. In other words, in the devotion to the Sacred Heart, atonement does not mean sacrifices as well as love but sacrifices which are the requirements of love itself, indispensable conditions for the purification, growth and manifestation of true love.

The famous mystical theologians of the eleventh and twelfth centuries, who were among the greatest venerators of the Sacred Heart, emphasized the aspect that Jesus alone could atone, since our love, being weak and insufficient, cannot be offered to the Father as atonement. For them this called for a particularly grateful love for the Sacred Heart, a fruitful love which would include the readiness to join Christ in the way of the cross.

Quite different was the emphasis that arose in the spirituality of St Francis of Assisi and St Catherine of Siena. There, in the foreground, was the configuration with Christ, especially in his compassion. Jesus has offered, in the name of humanity, such a fullness of atonement that from it derives an atoning value of the love of his disciples united with his passion and compassion.

That Jesus has atoned in the name of humanity does not dispense his followers from atonement. Rather, it enables and obliges us to realize in our own lives what Christ has offered in our name, in the name of humanity. It is this atoning love of ours that is still missing and is desired for the glory of the Father, for our own good and for the common good of the redeemed. This way of looking at our atoning vocation is part and parcel of the religious experience of St Margaret Mary. It is also the official interpretation of this devotion by the magisterium and the liturgy.

This vision follows the word of the Apostle of the gentiles: "It is now my happiness to suffer for you. This is my way of helping to complete, in my poor human flesh, the full tale of Christ's afflictions still to be endured, for the sake of his body which is the Church" (Col 1 : 24).

Christ has given evidence of his atoning love in all his life and in his passion and death. His love is so great that all his manifestations of love for the Father have absolute, infinite value. Yet he went all the way to the unsurpassable test of the cross. Insofar as Christ acted as head of the Church, there can be nothing lacking. But what is still to be completed is the appropriation of this same love by his disciples, tested by their readiness to bear the cross with Christ. His atoning love, made in the name of the Church, has to become flesh and blood in the Church, for the sake of humanity.

In view of the overflowing redemption in Christ, no member should be lacking in the matter of loving atonement. One who receives redemption and refuses to become an active, responsive member of the body of Christ deprives oneself of the dynamics of redemption and deprives also the Church and the world of his or her share in redemptive solidarity. This belongs to the very substance of the doctrine that "in him is plentiful redemption".

It should also be quite clearly said that atonement counts not in proportion to the heavy works of suffering and action but to the depth, strength and purity of love. The message of the book of Revelation to the "angel of Ephesus" acknowledges that the community has borne much turmoil for the sake of Christ, yet reproaches it: "You have lost your early love", whereas Thyatira receives approbation because "of late you have done even better than at first".

* * *

Dear Lord, I thank you and hope to be allowed to thank you in all eternity for your great love with which you have atoned for our sins and offered a worthy reparation to our heavenly Father. Despite all the misery and sin in the world we can rejoice, for from this earth, from our human family, the Father has received through you the most perfect response of love and loving atonement. We thank you for having done this in our name — in my name — in the name of all of us sinners. For us it is a great blessing that by your loving atonement you have shamed and challenged us for our lack of true love.

What value would our suffering and turmoil have if they were offered to our heavenly Father without your offering? And how could I ever dare to offer my weak and confused love to the all-holy God as atonement for my own and other people's sins, if it had not received its real value from your atonement and love for us.

I thank you, Jesus, for giving me a home in your loving heart and for accepting my love to offer, in union with yours, in atonement to the Father.

We praise you, our Redeemer, for, by your earthly life and your bitter passion, you have given value to our repentant love and to the sufferings which we accept in order to thank and praise you. Let us always be united with you. Help us to grow in your love, so that the Father can see you present in our efforts to purify our love and to make it a sign of thankful atonement.

12

Suffering in the light of the Sacred Heart of Jesus

> "We now see Jesus crowned with glory and honour because he suffered death, so that, by God's gracious will, in tasting death he should stand for us all. It was clearly fitting that God for whom and through whom all things exist should, in bringing many sons to glory, make the leader who delivers them perfect through sufferings. For a consecrating priest and those whom he consecrates are all of one stock; and that is why the Son does not shrink from calling men his brothers when he says . . . 'Here I am, and the children whom God has given me. . . And therefore he had to be made like these brothers of his in every way, so that he might be merciful and faithful as their high priest before God, to expiate the sins of the people!" (Heb 2:9–17).

> "Son though he was, he learned obedience in the school of suffering, and, once perfected, became the source of eternal salvation for all who obey him" (Heb 5:8–9).

IN the concentration camp in Auschwitz when the prisoners were particularly exposed to cruelty, one of them cried desperately to God: "Where are you now?" From the opposite corner another replied loudly: "Don't you see him, crucified here again, hanging on his cross?" This unusual dialogue between sufferers sheds much light on how the heart of Jesus takes us into the school of suffering, and also on the meaning of atonement.

Jesus' suffering has essentially a dimension of atonement for our sins; but how and why, no human tongue will ever be able to explain. It is the unfathomable mystery of God that he plunges so deeply into the suffering of a sinful world that he exposes himself, in his Son, even to calumny and torture by men. This profound mystery is symbolized in the Sacred Heart of Jesus. Pius XII wrote in his encyclical *Haurietis Aquas*: "Without penetrating into the mystical depths of Jesus' heart, nobody can understand anything about the mystery of the Crucified". Conversely, we may also say that nobody can be taken by Jesus into the mystical depths of his heart unless he is ready to express his love and gratitude to Jesus by sharing in his suffering.

In the history of theology we find many efforts to approach the mystery of atonement through Jesus. No one theory is satisfactory, since the mystery is greater than human reason. We can only stumble and turn our eyes to this divine secret from various angles.

The letter to the Hebrews is an irreplaceable gateway. The point is not at all that only such extreme suffering could fully atone for our sins. The key is rather that it was "fitting" in the divine plan of salvation that the Son of God, made man for our salvation, "one-of-us" in all things except sin, should also and in the fullest measure share in our suffering.

The logic of divine love and of the heart of Jesus is not, in the first place, that we should also suffer because Jesus suffered so much. Rather, the sublime thought is that since humanity, having loaded itself with sin, was inevitably exposed to all kinds of suffering, our redeemer and brother, Jesus, did not want to avoid suffering himself. Indeed, he, the God-Man with the most sensitive heart and mind, suffered more than anyone else. But what has redeemed us is not suffering as such but suffering as manifestation of the greatest love.

Thus Jesus taught us to transform suffering, to give it a new meaning of liberating love. Only then follows the second step in understanding. Since Jesus has suffered so much for us, it is "fitting" that his disciples also say "yes" to their suffering and take it as a sign of an all-embracing solidarity and of grateful love of Jesus who shows us the way.

A solidarity in sin makes others suffer senselessly, while a saving solidarity in Christ bears the burden of others. Thus we accept meaningful suffering, and make meaningful the suffering which otherwise would be meaningless.

It is in this way that we enter into the life-giving stream of salvation, into the redemptive work of Jesus. Receiving and sharing in this stream of human and divine love in the heart of Jesus, we become a part of redeeming solidarity.

The letter to the Hebrews boldly says that Jesus, "Son though he was, learned obedience". Even before suffering, and besides and beyond suffering, from the first moment of human consciousness, he was all loving obedience to the heavenly Father. He had total trust in the Father's love and wisdom. But in order to be fully "one-of-us" and to show us the way he also wanted to learn by the deepest experience what trusting and loving obedience is in the midst of the most intense suffering. What is decisive is not how much we have to suffer but that we learn from Jesus how great was the love with which he has given to suffering the new, redeeming meaning and dynamics.

The most cruel human suffering comes from the lovelessness by which people afflict each other. Nobody was as worthy of all love as Jesus was, yet nobody has been afflicted by such lovelessness. He has shown us how to take the poison out of such suffering, to break the vicious circle and to sanctify it by the most forgiving and healing love. And not only for his friends has he shown this greatest love by giving his life for them, but for his enemies also who crucified him. He died for us who, by our sins, have acted as enemies. Yet for all of us Jesus prays, "Father, forgive!"

His heart is physically pierced by the soldier's lance after being painfully pierced by men's loveless offences — by friends who should have stood under the cross with Mary and the beloved disciple, consoling him by grateful love.

Even by our lesser sins, which sometimes cause serious wounds to ourselves and others, we wound the heart of Jesus, though we do not deliberately turn away from him. The sensitive heart of Jesus was wounded not only by those who slandered him while he was hanging on the cross but also by those who had known him and dispassionately stayed away. We wound the body of Christ and the heart of Christ by so many sins of omission!

All this should be on our mind every time Jesus takes us into the school of his suffering. There we should never cease to thank him for having given new sense to suffering and for enabling us to do the same. Safe in his love, we praise him for having called us to have an active share in his work of redemption.

Faith, prompted by the power of the Spirit, is a gift which flows from the heart of Jesus. It follows from the very substance of living faith that in our sufferings and trials we entrust ourselves to Jesus, to the "thoughts of God's heart". Even the worst sufferings — those caused by our own sins or foolishness — are lightened if we trustfully believe that for those who love God everything turns to good. There is also the consoling awareness that, if our sufferings are accepted with faith and love, Jesus will make of them a fountain of grace for others, for in their transfigured meaning they flow from his heart, the fountain of all grace.

The sufferings of believers who dwell "in Christ", especially of those who are persecuted for the sake of faith and justice, are a part of the sufferings of the Church. It is she who, by sharing in the passion of Christ, prepares herself for "the wedding-supper of the Lamb" (Rev 19:9) and, indeed, has already begun to celebrate the unending wedding-feast.

Jesus interprets his passion and death in the words of his prayer: "I have made known thy name to the men whom thou didst give me" (Jn 17:6) and in the words: "The world must be shown that I love the Father and do exactly as he commands; so up, let us go forward" (Jn 14:31). As the members of the Church act and suffer in the same spirit as Jesus, with the same love for the Father and for the redeemed, then Jesus, through them, continues to show the world what redemption is, "that the world may believe" (Jn 17:22–23).

* * *

O divine and human heart of my Saviour, if I did not know and love you, the sufferings of humankind and my own sufferings would crush me. But turning my eyes to you, I can only praise you for having freed me from senseless suffering and from desperate death.

It is not you, beloved Redeemer, who has brought suffering into this world. Much of it comes from the sinfulness of the world. But in your unlimited love you decided to plunge into the ocean of our suffering in order to baptise and transfigure it with your own blood.

If, in faith and trust, we accept our share of suffering for the salvation of humankind in union with your death and resurrection, then we are no longer slaves of suffering and fearful of death. Our suffering no longer alienates us from each other; we are no longer oppressed by feelings of guilt. Rather, suffering becomes a salvific entrance for greater love of your heart and a liberating love for our neighbour.

Lord, increase my faith, my trust in you, my love, so that I can say "yes" to suffering and death, praising you for the meaning and redemptive power you give to them. And so I beg you to grant me, through the power of your Spirit, the strength to praise you unceasingly in the midst of suffering, for having united me and my suffering to your mission as redeemer of the world.

13

Consecration to the Sacred Heart of Jesus

> "I pray thee, not to take them out of the world, but to keep them from the evil one. They are strangers in the world, as I am. Consecrate them by the truth; thy word is truth. As thou hast sent me into the world, I have sent them into the world, and for their sake I now consecrate myself, that they too may be consecrated by the truth" (Jn 15–19).

FROM the very moment of the incarnation of the Word of God, the humanity of Jesus Christ is substantially consecrated to the glory of the Father and the salvation of humankind. The conscious life of Jesus is a constant "yes" to this mission and consecration. The high-priestly prayer offered to the Father in the presence of his chosen witnesses on the eve of his passion and death, the eve on which he gave us the perennial memorial of his death and resurrection, is his solemn consecration, the perfect expression of his loving dedication. And we, his disciples, are inserted into this consecration-prayer.

Jesus accepts us gratefully as gift of the Father. He loves us as belonging to the Father in spite of our striking imperfections. He makes us his friends and even a part of his love for the Father and consecrates us to be sharers in his own mission to the glory of the Father and redemption of mankind.

This, however, implies that through Jesus and in him we, his disciples, are made one. He prays: "Holy Father, protect by the power of thy name those whom thou hast given me, that they may be one, as we are one" (Jn 17:11). Then he continues: "that they may have my joy within them in full measure" (Jn 17:13). He, the Messiah, is "anointed with the oil of gladness" (Ps 45:7). "My joy" is sign of his consecration and readiness for fulfilment of his mission. The "gladness" makes him the "good news" in person. Hence, his disciples' participation in his mission implies their sharing in his joy, in the overflow of his love for the Father and in the fulfilment of his mission.

"Consecrate them by the truth; thy word is truth". The Word the Father sent us and the word Jesus speaks to us by his whole life is the truth that breathes love and bears fruit in love, joy and peace. That our heart and mind should be filled with this truth is an essential part of our election and dedication to share in Jesus' mission in the world. Then comes the solemn consecration prayer: "For them I consecrate myself, that they too may be consecrated by the truth".

The consecration to the Sacred Heart of Jesus, which belongs to the substance of this devotion, should be thoroughly understood in the light of Jesus' own consecration-prayer which stayed with him, in his heart, mind and will unto his last breath and his last heartbeat on the cross.

This prayer should be particularly dear to priests who, in a special way, are consecrated for the ministry of the word and the sacraments in configuration with Christ. But the Church rightly desires that all the faithful should consecrate themselves to the Heart of Jesus and thus to the heavenly Father. That means simply opening their hearts and wills to Jesus' own prayer of consecration in which he includes us all.

Already baptism, as sacrament of faith and faithfulness, is in itself a real and permanent consecration to the triune God and for an intimate belonging to Christ and his cause. The sacrament of confirmation is meant to bring this to completion through the anointment-consecration by the Holy Spirit, to show us clearly the road to a life consecrated for the kingdom of God. But all this needs to enter ever more into our conscious life of commitment.

The grace of God, freely granted, calls for a free and conscious response. This consecration has to enter fully into our fundamental option and to inform all levels of our conscious life. In this context of full convalidation of the fundamental option, the concept "heart" means the all-embracing, all-informing depth, the vital centre of our total response to God. And how could our "heart" become more alive if not by being conformed to the heart of Jesus, with his infinite love for the Father and for us?

Consecration to the Sacred Heart is, above all, a trustful prayer that our heart, mind and will, our memory and discernment may be formed by the love of Jesus, for which his opened heart, the heart of the risen Christ, stands as precious symbol. We consecrate ourselves to the service of his love, so that many will come to know the design of Jesus and the Father. In consecrating ourselves, we enter into Christ's own prayer of consecration and do so with great trust in the transforming power of his Spirit.

This is a profound self-commitment to strive at all times and in all events towards a holy life of redeemed and redeeming love as response to God's gracious action and appeal. It is our firm "yes" to the sanctifying and consecrating action of God, to our vocation to a saving solidarity of the redeemed, zeal for the salvation of all, constant battle against the solidarity of perdition.

The prayer of consecration to the Sacred Heart can and should bear personal traits since it is expected to rise from within our own heart. Furthermore, it is not just a matter of repetition, since our life situations also change. We offer here some models so that everyone will realize how different they are in many ways.

* * *

O Lord Jesus Christ, in union with the praise by which you honour God in all eternity, I desire to offer you this praise and these prayers. I implore your boundless mercy to grant me a contrite and devoted heart, a humble, chaste and zealous heart, a faithful and pure heart, a heart according to your heart, sanctified in your heart, drawn to your heart, a heart totally open to receive you: that I may not be attached to anything besides you, that I may not look for anything and not seek anything except you, that I may praise and thank you always, loving you always in all things and above all things.

(Prayer of Dionysius Ryckel, a Carthusian who died in 1471)

O golden gate, opened by the spear of Longinus, heart of the Saviour, here I enter into my safe refuge, the sure place of my beatitude.

To your opened heart, O Jesus, I offer, I entrust, I consecrate my heart, my soul, my body, my life and my death, all joys and sufferings of mine. Everything is yours and no longer mine, everything is yours entirely for ever and all eternity.

When my heart shall break in the hour of death, O living, wounded heart, receive me and enclose me wholly in you. May your wounded heart be the first thing I look upon and become my first repose.

(Consecration prayer of Trier, fifteenth century)

Most holy heart of Jesus, fullness of love, be my protection in life and pledge of eternal salvation. Be my strength in weakness and inconsistency. Be atonement for all the sins of my life.

O heart, gentle and kind, be our refuge in the hour of our death. Be our justification before God. Turn away from us punishment of just wrath.

O loving heart, in you I put all my trust. From our weakness we have to fear everything; from your love we hope everything. Blot out what could displease you; impress your love so deeply on our hearts that we never again forget you, that we can never be severed from you.

Lord and Saviour, for the sake of your love we plead: let our names be imprinted in your most holy heart. Let it be our happiness and honour to serve you in life and death.

(Prayer of St Margaret Mary Alacoque)

Most beloved Jesus, Saviour of humankind, look mercifully upon us who kneel in humility before your altar. Yours we are and yours we want to remain. That we might belong more intimately to you, each and all of us consecrate ourselves to your most holy heart.

Many have never come to know you, many have despised your commandments and have turned away from you. Kindest Jesus, have pity upon them and draw them all to your most holy heart.

Lord, king not only of the faithful who never have abandoned you, but also of your children who have gone astray, grant that soon they may return to the Father's house, so that they may not perish in misery and starvation.

Manifest yourself as king also of those who are deceived by

error or severed by schism. Call them back to the safe home of truth and unity of faith, so that there will be one sheepfold and one shepherd.

Show yourself as king of all who live imprisoned in the darkness of paganism. Lead them into the light of your reign.

Look mercifully upon the children of the people that you first have chosen. May your blood flow upon them as fountain of redemption and life.

Lord, grant your Church welfare, security and freedom. Grant all nations peace and order. Grant that, from one end of the earth to the other, the cry may resound: "Praise be to the divine heart through which salvation has come; praise and glory to him in all eternity".

(Consecration prayer of Pius XI, 1925)

"O Heart of Jesus, all love, I offer thee these humble prayers for myself and for all those who unite themselves with me in spirit to adore thee. O holiest Heart of Jesus, most lovely, I intend to renew and to offer to thee these acts of adoration and these prayers for me, a wretched sinner, and for all those who are associated in thy adoration, through all the moments while I breathe even to the end of my life.

I commend to thee, O my Jesus, holy Church, thy dear spouse, and our true mother, the souls which practise justice, and all poor sinners, the afflicted, the dying, and all men. Let not thy blood be shed for them in vain.

Finally, deign to apply it in relief of the souls in purgatory, those in particular who have practised in the course of their life this holy devotion of adoring thee".

(Consecration prayer for religious)

Most kind Lord and Master, when before your passion you solemnly consecrated yourself for the salvation of the world, you graciously included me in this consecration. The blessing of this consecration has abundantly reached my heart in baptism, in confirmation and in Holy Communion as a stream of grace by which you have introduced me into the riches of your loving heart and united me with your body and your blood shed for me.

I thank you that, time and again, you have touched my heart by your grace and called me to intimate friendship. I thank you for all the graces you have lavished upon me when I offered you my religious vows. I thank you for having accepted my offering in spite of my weakness, and for consecrating me by your love and accompanying me lovingly on all my ways.

I now renew my consecration to confirm and deepen my baptismal and religious vows, with deep sorrow that so many times I did not fulfil them with unbroken fidelity; but at the same time, I do it with great trust in your forgiving and healing love.

Lord, accept me as I am and make me what you want me to be. Take away from me everything that stands in the way of your love and grant me everything that leads me to the fullest union with you.

I thank you, most loving Master, for having called me to be a witness to your love for all and thank you particularly for enabling me to love and serve those who are poor and unloved, so that they may feel a ray of your own love.

In this renewed consecration I pray especially for my community. Make us all one in your heart, so that together we can help the world to find you, the saviour of all.

O Mary, mother of our Redeemer and our mother, you are nearest to the heart of your Son. At each moment of your life you have confirmed your "yes" to your great vocation. Pray for me that I may hold fast to this consecration.

(Consecration prayer of Cardinal John Henry Newman, 1849)

14

Consecration of the whole world to the Sacred Heart of Jesus

> "You are merciful to all, because you can do all things
> and overlook men's sins so that they can repent.
> Yes, you love all that exists,
> you hold nothing of what you have made in abhorrence,
> for had you hated anything, you would not have formed it.
> And how, had you not willed it, could a thing persist,
> how be conserved if not called forth by you?
> You spare all things because they are yours, Lord,
> lover of life,
> You whose imperishable spirit is in all.
> Little by little, therefore, you correct those who offend,
> You admonish and remind them of how they have sinned,
> so that they may abstain from evil and trust in you, Lord"
> (Wis 11:23, 12:2).

GOD cannot but love the world created by him. Yet we are astonished that he loves a world that he sees entangled in sin. We are amazed by his mercy when he looks on a humankind that, through rebellion against its creator, has afflicted itself with terrible misery.

Looking at Jesus, the Redeemer of the world, we are astonished even more than the author of the book of Wisdom. Forever Jesus loves the world for whose redemption the Father sent him and for which he has shed his heart's blood. In his consecration prayer (John 17) Jesus shares his own consecration with his disciples whom he is sending into the world to make known to all people the love with which he, the Redeemer, loves the world. The disciples are called to be holy, to be one in heart and mind, so that the world may receive a taste of the love with which the Father sent his only Son to redeem it.

In his high-priestly prayer Jesus gives two quite different connotations to the word "world". This becomes evident in the context and through the context. There is the "godless world", the leading class in Jerusalem, the religious and political leaders at that moment, who obstinately reject the call to salvation and to grateful love because of their individual and collective egotism and lust for power. The disciples have to be aware of that godless world, of the temptations that arise from it and the persecution which comes from it against those who proclaim the gospel in its fullness.

And there is the other world about which Jesus speaks insofar as it is redeemed by him and for which he is ready to die although it is a world in which good and bad are terribly interwoven. This world will always be in need of God's mercy and of a convincing witness not only from some individual disciples of Jesus but from the community of disciples who, by their oneness in heart and mind, reflect the love and saving purpose of Christ.

The traditional devotion to the Sacred Heart received an important clarification and broadening of horizon through Leo XIII, who in his encyclical *Annum Sacrum* called for the consecration of the whole world to the Sacred Heart of Jesus. Thus certain privatizing tendencies are clearly rejected. Jesus wants to draw to himself all human hearts so that they may join him in his all-inclusive love as sharers of his mission to be redeemer and deliverer of humanity. Jesus cannot accept the love of a heart that closes itself in its individual concerns. The Church knows that she is chosen, sent and conquered by the heart of Jesus for the salvation of the world.

The consecration of the whole world to the Sacred Heart unmasks also the deviation of activists who think they are able to set the world free by their own forces, by manipulation of its cultural, economic and socio-political structures. These manipulators pervert themselves and all fundamental human relationships. Since their trust is only in themselves and their manipulative skills, they easily tend to violence, class hatred and war, ideology against ideology, nation against nation.

If anyone were to know the best political constitution, the best form of economic life, the ideal structures of culture, and besides had the skill and power to manipulate humanity for his designs, the world would not become any better. In the hands of manipulated manipulators everything would turn out wrong.

The most urgent and, indeed, the only effective remedy to heal public life is the change of heart that would liberate us from individual and collective egotism by conversion to true love and justice. Ultimately, this means the turning of hearts to the fountain of love that is opened to us in the heart of Jesus.

Already in the Old Testament, prophets — especially Jeremiah and Ezekiel — spoke of the renewed heart and of a "new covenant" in a coupling or "tandem" sense. Together they could form a new saving-solidarity among men and women, first in view of the sacred "remnant" but through it reaching all humankind. The sacred "remnant" are those who, "one in heart and mind", turn to the Redeemer of the world.

The consecration of the world to the Sacred Heart of Jesus, through individual communities and the whole Church, is a solemn act of commitment to redemptive solidarity, a commitment to the mission received from the Divine Master to be "salt for the earth", "light to the world". No one can join in this consecration without a readiness to shoulder his part of co-responsibility for the salvation of the world.

There is a clear dynamics of truth in this co-responsibility for the welfare and salvation of the whole of humanity in view of the Sacred Heart of the Redeemer of the world. What humanity needs more than anything else are loving hearts, healthy human relationships, people who radiate peace and love, who build bridges between heart and heart, enkindling light and warmth and leading to an all-inclusive holistic vision. The basic symbol of this wholeness and solidarity is "the heart of man".

Since Leo XIII Catholic social teaching has insisted on the inseparability of change of heart and change of social conditions. We have to be at the same time committed to both dimensions, but the change of heart has priority on the level of value. It is the healthy and indispensable source of all effective efforts to change the economic, cultural, social and political conditions of the world for the better. There is no chance to obtain a healthy economic world order without sincere intentions and motives by all who are willing to work for it. Surely we need structural remedies too, but they fulfil their purpose only when the hearts of people meet in sincere dedication to healing justice.

Those who, with their local and the universal Church, consecrate themselves to the Sacred Heart have to be aware of the ambiguity of the "world" and of their own heart. Both are in need of redemption. Only with great trust in the Redeemer of the world can we fight against this dual ambiguity. The consecration will, therefore, imply persistent prayer for the healing of our own heart — of all human relationships — and commitment to the healing of public life.

One who authentically venerates the Sacred Heart never thinks of self-fulfilment or only of saving his own soul. He is consecrated to the salvation of the whole world. This weakens in no way our striving for personal wholeness and holiness; rather, it strengthens it in the total context of a saving solidarity. We pray then for *them*: "For all humankind I consecrate myself, that they too may be consecrated, truly redeemed".

Consecration of the world, as a solemn self-commitment to the salvation of the world by believing communities, does not allow a superficial optimism but allows even less a dangerous pessimism which weakens all the inner resources. The heart of Jesus, pierced and opened, contradicts the pessimist's conclusion that the world is a hopeless case and that flight from it would be the better course. One who truly venerates the Heart of Jesus neither disembarks nor cries "SOS". The only purpose of one's effort to gain a healthy distance from the lures of the world is to become a purified, sincere, healthy and healing presence in the world. The healing of public life needs honesty in the fullest sense: absolute sincerity and generosity.

* * *

Oh my Saviour, Saviour of the world, the more I am touched by a ray of your love, the more I experience deliverance from narrowness and cowardliness. In your divine and human heart there is room for the whole world. I realize now how impossible it is to love you without joining you in your all-inclusive love.

This gives new meaning to my commitment to your heart. It becomes ever more a "yes" to your consecrating prayer at the Last Supper. I thank you for thus consecrating yourself for the salvation of the world and for including us, your disciples, in this consecration. I thank you for sending us out into the world with the same love and the same mandate of love and peace with which your heavenly Father sent you into this world.

I praise you for letting your light shine upon us so much that in your light we poor creatures can become "light to the world".

Drawn irresistibly by your consecration to the salvation of the world, I renounce all the selfishness of my heart and of any group. O Lord, free me from all self-seeking interests. I want to do everything that will help people to open their hearts to one another in mutual respect, justice and compassion. I long for a heart full of compassion for the suffering and of dedication to the poor and unloved. I do not intend to write off the rich and powerful of this world; I want only to bring to them and to all who enjoy influence in public life the saving message that they too are redeemed and can join in valuable actions for the healing of public life. Help me to convince them that they are not irrevocably condemned to be enslaved by the voracious gods of riches and power. I want to shout from the rooftops to the heart of all people that they can be freed for the work of justice and peace by redeeming love.

O Sacred Heart of my Redeemer and Redeemer of the world, I would never dare to join the Church in the consecration of the whole of humanity if I would not put all my trust in you. Cleanse, broaden and strengthen our hearts so that we may truly become what you want us to be: light to the world.

15

Consecration of the family to the Sacred Heart of Jesus

> "Let the Holy Spirit fill you: speak to one another in psalms, hymns and songs; sing and make music in your hearts to the Lord; and in the name of our Lord Jesus Christ give thanks every day for everything to our God and our Father. Be subject to one another out of reverence for Christ. . . Husbands, love your wives, as Christ also loved the Church and gave himself up for it, to consecrate it, cleansing it by water and word, so that he might present the Church to himself all glorious, with no stain or wrinkle or anything of the sort, but holy and without blemish. In the same way men also are bound to love their wives, as they love their own body" (Eph 5 : 18–28).

THE family is a most privileged place where heart meets heart and heart speaks to heart. Therefore it is in accord with the "logic of the heart" that christian families consecrate themselves to the Sacred Heart of Jesus. Husband and wife, parents and children, brothers and sisters can love each other as redeemed people with a love that has its fountain in the heart of Jesus. Loving familial relationships and authentic veneration of the Sacred Heart call for each other and foster each other.

A christian family, which consecrates itself to the Sacred Heart as a whole, intends to participate in Jesus' self-consecration, which also included the intention that the whole family of his disciples might be "truly consecrated". It is not too difficult to discern the essential traits. In his consecration prayer Jesus sees his disciples as a precious gift of the heavenly Father to him, and he on his part makes of himself a total gift to his disciples, even to death on a cross. In each eucharistic celebration we relive this mutuality: Jesus accepts us as gift of the Father and makes a gift of himself to us, and we are enabled by his Spirit to entrust ourselves as a grateful gift to him. Thus our consecration is confirmed and deepened.

Marital love reaches its sublime nobility in the fundamental experience of husband and wife. God has given us our mutual love; he has given each of us to the other as his gift, and in our mutual love he, the giver of all good gifts, is lovingly present. In the measure that spouses love each other, they see each other as a wonderful gift.

From this perspective the Second Vatican Council does not speak of marriage as a "contract" but as a "covenant in mutual self-bestowal". It is a covenant of mutual love inserted into the new and everlasting covenant between Christ and his Church.

Good parents honour their children as gifts of God and as the crowning of their mutual love. Parents transmit life in its fully human value only when they greet their children as sharers in the mutuality of their love or, let us say, as concelebrants of the everlasting covenant of love. Happy the children who, day by day, experience that their parents, by their words and conduct, let them feel: "we are glad to have you; it is wonderful that God has given you to us; it is happiness that we live for each other!" If this experience is vitally present, then it will be quite natural that brothers and sisters, too, will accept and affirm each other as a gift which has more value than all material things.

The christian family that takes its orientation from the heart of Jesus is the most valuable school for learning redeemed and redeeming love for each other and then also for others. The mutual respect and the submission to each other and their common good have their model in the loving obedience of Jesus to his heavenly Father and his loving dedication to his "new family" — the redeemed — and in the grateful love of the Church for her Saviour.

The spirit of a good christian family is marked by praise and thanksgiving. Family prayer and praise of God and of our Lord Jesus Christ confirm and deepen the mutual bonds of loving reverence. It helps to discover in each other the rich inner resources for shared growth in whatever is good, beautiful and true, and for mutual encouragement in life's battles against unfavourable inclinations.

In the shared praise and thanksgiving grows the vital intuition that God accepts each member of this family as he or she is, and takes each of them by the hand to guide him or her according to his design on the way to maturity when the full stature of Christ becomes visible in them. Thus they grow in redeemed co-humanity for each other and for all God's household.

In this spirit of faith and adoration the members of the family become ever more consciously companions for each other on the road to wholeness and holiness. They learn together from Jesus the great commandment, "Love each other as I have loved you" (Jn 15: 12). As the Apostle expresses it, they learn "to bear the burden of each other and thus to fulfil the law of Christ" (Gal 6: 2). The stronger ones will help the weaker ones and respect them. In a healthy family there will be patience for each other. And when difficulties arise in a member of the family, he or she will be helped not only by kind correction but even more by pre-existing trust — just as Jesus acts with us.

If an entire family consecrates itself to the Sacred Heart, as several popes have recommended, this can greatly contribute to a clear and purposeful orientation for mutual love and creative co-responsibility. But it implies also a firm orientation of the family as a whole to participate in the work of redemption, of healing people and healing public life. They intend to radiate kindness, goodness, generosity, co-responsibility in their environment among friends and neighbours.

* * *

Beloved Saviour, we thank you, for, by your life in the holy family of Nazareth, you have consecrated the christian family and have made it a privileged school of holiness in mutual love. Coming from the heart of the Father, you chose to learn human love by experience in the bosom of a human family. Your whole life is marked by the love you have received from your mother and from St Joseph. You were happy to love them in return and thus to enrich your beloved ones. We cannot think of your heart's love for people and of your compassionate teaching without being reminded of the family wherein all this unfolded as you grew in age and wisdom.

We thank you also for the mutual love of our parents, which was the fountain of their love for us. We thank you for the love and affirmation received from our brothers and sisters, re-echoing the love of our parents. Grant us that this wealth of love may become fruitful in all our relationships and especially in the strength to love unloved people.

Most loving heart of Jesus, when you consecrated yourself to the Father for our salvation, you prayed that we too might be consecrated in truth. So we consecrate our family to you and, with you, to the Father. Consecrated to your loving heart we intend to help each other faithfully to grow in love for you and for each other.

Consecrated to your heart we shall watch over the sincerity and fidelity of our love. We will help each other to discover the inner resources in each of us and all of us for growth in love and responsibility. Together we want to learn to reach out to others, to accept and give friendship and to associate ourselves with others in endeavours for the welfare and salvation of all.

Lord, accept our consecration, accept our mutual love. Cleanse and strengthen it and make it a source of blessing for many.

F

16

Streams of living water

> "On the last and greatest day of the festival Jesus stood and cried aloud, 'If anyone is thirsty let him come to me; whoever believes in me, let him drink'. As Scripture says, 'Streams of living water shall flow out from within him'. He was speaking of the Spirit which believers in him would receive later; for the Spirit had not yet been given, because Jesus had not yet been glorified" (Jn 7:37–39).

> "One of the soldiers stabbed his side with a lance, and at once there was a flow of blood and water. This is vouched for by an eye-witness, whose evidence is to be trusted" (Jn 19:34).

THE symbol of "streams of living water", which first have to flow from the pierced heart of the Redeemer before they can flow from believers, belongs to the heritage of the whole history of the devotion to the Sacred Heart. It is one of its biblical foundations which attracted many hearts. With the opening of the heart of the Redeemer, who with his last breath has entrusted his Spirit to the Father, the first act of glorification of the Father is accomplished. It will be followed by the glorification of the Son, through the Father, in Christ's resurrection and in the effusion of the Holy Spirit.

From the fountain of salvation believers drink the great gift of redemption, the Holy Spirit, who opens our hearts for redeemed love, flooding them with the overflow of boundless love from the heart of Jesus. "God's love has flooded our inmost heart through the Holy Spirit he has given us" (Rom 5:5). Urgently Jesus invites us to drink from this fountain, not only enough to quench our thirst but also to enable us to become for others a fountain of saving love.

For this great encyclical on the Sacred Heart Pius XII chose as opening words "*Haurietis Aquas*", from the text of the prophet: "You will draw waters joyfully from the springs of salvation" (Is 12:3). This is cause for rejoicing, thanksgiving and praise: "Cry out for joy and gladness, you dwellers in Zion, for great in the midst of you is the Holy One of Israel" (Is 12:6). The image reminds us of Moses whom God told to call for living water from a rock. And Paul says: "They all drank from the supernatural rock that accompanied their travels — and that rock was Christ" (1 Cor 10:4).

In his encyclical Pius XII says: "This connection between divine love, which should inflame the hearts of believers, and the Holy Spirit, as indicated by Scripture, characterizes splendidly the inmost essence of the devotion which is offered to the most holy heart of Jesus".

The first thing for us to do, therefore, is to quench our thirst for redeeming love at the fountain of salvation, as Jesus invited us to do: "If anyone is thirsty let him come to me!" The Holy Spirit as well as the ministry of salvation in the Church give to this invitation a never-ending echo; and everyone who has tasted the streams of living water will eagerly pass on to others this same invitation. " 'Come!' say the Spirit and the bride. 'Come!' let each hearer reply. Come forward, you who are thirsty, accept the water of life, a free gift to all who desire it" (Rev 22:17).

Jesus himself, who on the cross was both humiliated and exalted, meets us with his abundant love, the source of life. "The lamb who is at the heart of the throne will be their shepherd and will guide them to the springs of the water of life" (Rev 7:17).

The Holy Spirit, the third Person in the Holy Trinity, is the personified gift by which the Father eternally gives himself to his Word, his Son, and the Word returns his love and himself as gift to the Father. In his humanity Jesus is anointed and sent by the Spirit for the work of redemption. In the power of the same Spirit Jesus makes himself on the cross a sacrificial gift to the Father for our sake. And with the flow of blood and water from his opened heart, he becomes the fountain of the gift of the Holy Spirit for us.

By the same power of the Spirit by which Jesus has made himself a sin-offering for us sinners, he gives himself in the Eucharist as a source of everlasting love for us. And the admirable circle becomes perfect in that Jesus sends us the Holy Spirit, from the Father, to enable us to give our hearts and entrust ourselves to the Father in union with Jesus. Thus all our life becomes an expression of grateful love, of perennial praise for such an undeserved gift.

"Superabundant redemption" manifests itself particularly when those who have appeased their thirst at the fountain of the water of life and are captured by the love of Jesus become one with Christ, so that "streams of living water shall flow out from within them".

It is clear biblical teaching that nobody can have a vital share in the love of the Redeemer without joining him actively in his love for all. The gifts of the Spirit cannot be buried in a selfish heart. Through unceasing thanksgiving for these gifts our hearts will become more and more conformed to the heart of Jesus, Redeemer of the world. As a consequence, during all our life we shall urge all who are thirsty to come to Jesus and to drink from his love.

The consecration of ourselves and of the world to the Heart of Jesus must be seen in this light. If we are consecrated by the Holy Spirit to the love of the Redeemer of the world, we consciously accept our mission: "As thou hast sent me into the world, I have sent them into the world, and for their sake I now consecrate myself" (Jn 17: 18–19). Jesus makes it clear that this mission and consecration come to us as a transforming, renewing power of the Spirit: "Jesus repeated, 'Peace be with you!' and said, 'As the Father sent me, so I send you'. Then he breathed on them, saying, 'Receive the Holy Spirit' " (Jn 20: 20–22).

What we and the whole world most urgently need is that love which flows from the heart of Jesus, pierced for us and glorified by the Father. The beginning of the way of salvation is to have a great thirst for this love, without which we cannot be salt for the earth and light to the world. If we are alert to how much the world needs this greatest of all gifts, this awareness will increase our own longing and striving. It is this that matters for all of us.

* * *

Most loving Lord and Master, the terrible thirst which you suffered when you were losing the last drops of your precious blood is a heart-breaking symbol of your heart's thirst to share with us the riches of your love and your redemption. We thank you for constantly inviting us, through your own voice from the cross, through the voice of the Spirit and the "bride", and through the voices of all who venerate your heart, to drink thirstily at the fountain of salvation so that the water of life can flow for others from within us.

Send forth your Spirit to awaken in us this thirst. Let your thirst become ours; let your love become our love for all the redeemed, so that all may come to experience this love and become ever more thirsty for a greater love.

Lord Jesus, you have told us that "if two of you agree on earth about any request you have to make, that request will be granted by my heavenly Father" (Mt 18: 19). We know that we can pray with full trust if we look at what your heart desires most for us. So we come to pray not for small things but for the greatest of all gifts: that you draw us so much to your heart that our longing may be to see all people drawn to this same love. Then there will be goodness and peace throughout the world, and you can hand us all over to the Father as your gift, "and the Father will be glorified in the Son" (Jn 14: 13).

Lord Jesus, when blood and water flowed from your pierced heart on the cross, so did all the streams of salvation. We beg you, send us your Holy Spirit to renew our hearts, to cleanse them and inflame them with your love: love for you, love for our brothers and sisters all over the world. Grant us a joyful, grateful and strong faith, for only from within can streams of the water of life flow from true believers to others.

17

The Heart of Jesus and the Church

> "Christ also loved the Church and gave himself up for her, to consecrate her, cleansing her by water and word, so that he might present the Church to himself all glorious, with no stain or wrinkle or anything of the sort, but holy and without blemish" (Eph 5 : 25–27).

THE Old Testament shows that God's election is directed to the people as a whole, to the individual more as a member of a people. God is the "spouse", the "good shepherd" of his people. In the New Testament these images come to bear on the relationship of Christ to his Church. The twelve apostles, the cornerstones of the Church, point to a continuity with the once-united twelve tribes of the chosen people.

The covenant sealed by the blood of the Redeemer, which we celebrate in the Eucharist as the people of this covenant, is the covenant of love with the Church, but in such a way that each member counts in his or her uniqueness. The Church as a whole points to all humankind.

Since the time of the Church fathers, theology has held that the Church is born from the opened heart of Jesus. His heart's blood is her dowry. To her the streams of salvation flow, the gift of the Spirit. Or, to speak without image: in an ineffable and faithful love Jesus has chosen the Church for no merit on her part but only out of his gratuitous love. He has given her life by his redemption, has called her into being by his creative word and has bestowed on her the promise to abide with her unto the end of history.

The Church can understand herself, her worth and her mission only as coming from the love of Jesus Christ. Hence her first and fundamental task is to learn to know and to love Jesus. Thereby she learns to love all people in union with Jesus' own love. She is the sacrament of salvation insofar as she makes visible in her members, her charisms and her ministries, her constitution, liturgy and even in her laws and their application, the love of Jesus and her love for him. She is called to radiate that love. It should flow from her as a stream of living water.

For this purpose an authentic devotion to the Sacred Heart is most fitting and fruitful. It is a tremendous challenge to the Church and her self-understanding, for, in this devotion of devotions, what matters above all is to be touched and moved by the love of the Sacred Heart and to love, with Jesus, the heavenly Father and all the redeemed.

This devotion is also fruitful for an ongoing examination of conscience which concerns the Church as a whole in each of her aspects and in each of her members. The result is often a deep sorrow or even a profound shock that we, as members and widespread parts of the Church, respond so poorly to that love which has chosen us and gives us life. Our reaction should lead us to humble confession and at the same time to grateful praise, "for his mercy is without end" despite our partial lack of fidelity. But, of course, this praise makes sense only when we renew our purpose to respond to this divine fidelity through a much more steadfast faithfulness. We should no longer be a source of disappointment for Jesus.

The Church is meant to be a source of joy for her divine spouse. Jesus rejoices that the Father has entrusted her to him as his gift. He rejoices about those who humbly and gratefully respond to his love. He knows not only the canonized saints but also all the hidden saints and the many who, in spite of enormous obstacles, are striving for total conversion. He looks with kindness upon the poor sinners who have learned to put all their trust in him. There is great rejoicing in heaven for each of them, and that means also rejoicing in the heart of Jesus. Jesus looks with delight on the preaching of conversion through the Church, if it is coupled with her readiness for ongoing renewal of all aspects of her life. The heart of Jesus welcomes the new impetus in many parts of christianity towards reunion of the separated parts, especially if these efforts are marked by great humility.

But the Church has also cost the heart of Jesus many pains. Since he so deeply loved his disciples, their stubborness and rivalry, their resistance against his real mission as the Suffering Messiah saddened him many times. Time and again when he explained his mission to free mankind from pride and arrogance by humble service, his disciples immediately began disputing about which of them would play the most important role. Even when Jesus had washed their feet and explained what this was meant to teach them, they refused what it implied. These and many other occasions must have given Jesus a shocking picture of all that would go wrong in future times in his Church with people who would be calling themselves "christians".

The extreme suffering of Jesus' heart and soul on the Mount of Olives on the eve of his passion was increased by the apathy and drowsiness of his disciples from whom he should have been able to expect sympathy and consolation. But these are not just past events. They are repeated also in our time, even by ourselves who give so little thought to being a source of joy for all, to the glory of Jesus Christ.

If we look at the heart of Jesus or if we see his eyes turned to us, we shall not be tempted to make ourselves judges of the "Church", forgetting that we are a part of her and a partial cause of her weaknesses and her distress. It is you and I, members of the Church, who harm the Church by our sins and negligences. We hide her true countenance from people. Jesus must be most painfully surprised if then we dare to play judge over the Church.

It is true that a deep knowledge and love of Jesus call for self-criticism in the Church, including its office-holders. We should suffer with Jesus when we see partial failures in the Church, failures of her mission caused by lack of holiness. But if it is really the love of Jesus that seizes and awakens us, we shall always begin with criticism of ourselves. And our critical awareness of the imperfections of structures and of office-holders in the Church should join Christ's mercy and compassion and increase our own striving for holiness.

When we look at the Church in the sight of Jesus, we shall be ever more gratefully aware of all the good we have received and still receive in the Church and from the Church. If we realize how difficult it is for institutional traditions to change and to enter fully into Jesus' mandate for unity in diversity, we shall praise the Lord even more that so much healthy reform has been possible. Especially, we shall praise him for the saints who teach us by their lives that individual conversion and fruitful commitment to Church renewal are possible if we put our trust in the Lord.

Our relationship with the Church — as her members — is healthy if we consider everything in the light of the love of Jesus for his Church. We see the Church arising from his pierced heart, flowing from it with the blood and water released by the lance. It is, then, clear that we cannot drink from the water of salvation if we bypass the Church, her ministry of the word and her sacraments.

Our wounded relationships with the Church will be healed if we look at her in this light. St Augustine writes about the heart opened for us: "The gateway to life was opened. Through it flow the sacraments of the Church. . . Nothing has more power to heal than this wound. Through this gate comes salvation, through it we enter into the reign of love".

* * *

All-loving Saviour, we praise you for your great love with which you have espoused your Church in all her poverty. You have accepted her as a gift designed by the heavenly Father. You have shed the last drop of your heart's blood for her. She has an abiding place in your heart.

I want to unite myself with all the grateful love which you have received from your Church, from her saints and penitents. With all the Church I praise you for your boundless faithfulness and the healing powers flowing from your heart to heal our partial faithlessness. I unite my sorrow and penitence with all the saint-penitents of the past and present, with all who venerate your Sacred Heart, especially those who knew how to offer you atonement in union with the atonement which you have offered for us to your Father.

I want to joint you in your great and steadfast love for your Church and to learn from you how to love her with the love with which you love her unto the end of time. Help me by your grace gratefully to accept my place in the Church and to serve her faithfully and sincerely.

Assist your Church to grow in the knowledge and love of your Sacred Heart. Bless her so that she may be able to lead all people to love you.

18

The Heart of Jesus and the Sacrament of Love

> "Jesus answered, 'I tell you this; the truth is, not that Moses gave you the bread from heaven, but that my Father gives the real bread from heaven. The bread that God gives comes down from heaven and brings life to the world'. They said to him, 'Sir, give us this bread now and always'. Jesus said to them, 'I am the bread of life. Whoever comes to me shall never be hungry, and whoever believes in me shall never be thirsty' " (Jn 6:32–35).

HISTORY shows that devotion to the Sacred Heart of Jesus and a great love for the Eucharist are inseparable. This is most evident in the lives of St Gertrude and St Mechtilde. Their devotion to the Sacred Heart had its centre in the liturgy. The celebration of the Eucharist inspired them to contemplate and to praise the loving heart of Jesus who, seated at the right hand of the Father, constantly intercedes for us. Jesus, who gave us this memorial of his sacrificial and atoning love, is now present in the Eucharist to give us the wonderful pledge of the love of his heart. It is especially in the Eucharist that he offers us, as it were, an "exchange of heart", conforming our heart to his heart.

The adoration of Jesus in the Eucharist and union with him in praise of the Father are at the very centre of St John Eudes' devotion to the Sacred Heart. His zeal to see the mystery of Jesus' Heart honoured by a special feast and liturgy sparked also his emphasis on an atoning love for Jesus who, in this great sacrament of the Eucharist, deserves our grateful love.

Only with deep sorrow can we think of how many people remain ungrateful and even directly dishonour the Lord in the Eucharist. St John Eudes calls for special atonement for all the sins against the eucharistic heart of Jesus. This atonement, centred in a grateful and sacrificial love, is ready to offer everything that love demands in reparation for the sins of ingratitude. And St John Eudes is well aware that our atonement can have value only in union with the sacrifice of Christ, a union of heart and mind to which Jesus invites us and makes possible for us in the Eucharist.

The spirituality of St Margaret Mary Alacoque shows a similar emphasis. She is convinced that souls wholly captured by the eucharistic love of Jesus can atone validly and, by their adoring and generous love, can somehow provide a balance for the terrible coldness and hardness of so many hearts. She also promoted the liturgical celebration of the mystery of the Sacred Heart with the same zeal as St John Eudes.

It should be noted here that these classical representatives of the devotion to the Sacred Heart show no privatizing tendency. On the contrary, they express a saving solidarity. We should also remember that John Eudes and Margaret Mary Alacoque helped greatly to overcome Jansenism which, by its rigorism, alienated many christians from Holy Communion and from trust in the merciful love of the Redeemer.

St Alphonsus, the most efficacious protagonist against jansenistic rigorism and coldness of heart, was another great promoter of the devotion to the Sacred Heart and its liturgical celebration. He extols particularly the permanent Presence in the Eucharist as a sign of the invincible love of the heart of Jesus. He feels that for those who have received the body and blood of Christ with great trust and devotion, the silent proximity of Jesus becomes the eloquent language of love, a perennial memorial of the crucified love and a continuous formation of a grateful memory. He sees the daily visit to the Blessed Sacrament as an expression of a grateful memory and of constant praise because Jesus never forgets us.

This great eulogist of the eucharistic memorial also considers the human memory to be a foundational gift before intellect and will. Through a grateful memory God inserts us into the history of salvation, opens to us the treasures of the past, enriches the present and provides dynamics for the orientation of the future.

Finding our blissful abode with Jesus in the Blessed Sacrament, indeed, in his very heart, is an anticipation of heaven and constant guidance on the road to it. In the sacrament of loving union Alphonsus finds the Divine Physician, the Good Shepherd who nourishes in us the effective and faithful sentiments of friendship, trust, love and the joy to be near him.

The most ardent promoters of the liturgical celebration of the mystery of the Sacred Heart have held that this devotion should be seen wholly in the light of the liturgy, and vice versa. St Alphonsus, like other great venerators of the Sacred Heart, was a persistent promoter of the practice of frequent Holy Communion, not only for religious but equally for all lay people. He was convinced that rigorists — out of respect for the Holy One, as they asserted — did not really know the merciful love of the heavenly Father and the loving heart of the Redeemer.

We do not go to Communion in order to be rewarded for our virtue. Rather, we accept joyfully the divine invitation since we know the gracious, merciful and healing love of Jesus and yearn to love him in return. As we receive from him healing and strength, we long all the more to grow in our love for him and, through him, in our love for our neighbour, since he alone is the source of redeemed and redeeming love.

In Holy Communion Jesus, in the power of the Holy Spirit, gives himself with the same love with which he offered himself up for us on the cross. At the same time he shares with us the gift of the Spirit so that we become able to reciprocate his love and give ourselves totally to him. We ask him to make us wholly his own and to conform our hearts to his. Thus his consecrating action becomes reality in our life.

We join Jesus in his high-priestly prayer, "for them I consecrate myself, that they too may be consecrated in truth". In trustful prayer of supplication we open ourselves to this grace and fecundity of Holy Communion wherein heart reposes in heart. With a renewed heart we come closer to the beatitude assured to those who are "pure in heart". A grateful memory will then help us to watch over the purity of our motives and intentions.

In the Eucharist we celebrate the sacrificial love of Jesus, the unsurpassable love which he made visible in his bitter passion and the sacrifice of his life, while praying that this sacrifice may touch and change our hearts and inspire in us a generous and atoning love. As we praise the Father for having prepared this supreme offering for us, made by Jesus once and for all, our hearts open more and more to the grace that transforms us and makes us an acceptable offering in union with Christ. Gradually we learn to free ourselves from everything that stands in the way of our union with the sacrificial and atoning love of Jesus.

In the Eucharist Jesus prepares the festive banquet for his friends, a pledge of the heavenly banquet and everlasting feast of love and joy. Thus we come to a better understanding of his invitation: "Come to me, all whose work is hard, whose load is heavy; and I will give you relief" (Mt 11:28); "Come forward, you who are thirsty; accept the water of life, a free gift to all who desire it" (Rev 22:17). And we respond with all our heart: "Come, Lord Jesus" (Rev 22:21).

* * *

"O most sacred, most loving heart of Jesus, thou art concealed in the Holy Eucharist, and thou dost beat for us still. Now as then thou sayest, *Desiderio desideravi* — 'With desire I have desired'. I worship thee then with all my best love and awe, with my fervent affection, with my most subdued, most resolved will.

O my God, when thou dost condescend to suffer me to receive thee, to eat and drink thee, and thou for a while takest up thy abode within me, O make my heart beat with thy heart. Purify it of all that is earthly, all that is proud and sensual, all that is hard and cruel, of all perversity, of all disorder, of all deadness. So fill it with thee, that neither the events of the day nor the circumstances of the time may have power to ruffle it; but that in thy love and thy fear it may have peace".

(Prayer of Cardinal John Henry Newman)

"O my Jesus, you have not refused to give me your blood and body, your life; and how, then, can I refuse to give you my miserable heart? May that never happen! My dear Redeemer, I offer you everything, all my will; accept it and do with it what you will. I have nothing and can do nothing, but this I have to give you: my heart which you have given me, which nobody can steal from me; I may lose things, my blood, my life, but not my heart. With this heart I can love you and will love you.

O my God, teach me to forget myself; teach me how to come to your pure love; in your goodness you have already inspired in me a great desire for this love. I feel in myself a strong decision to please you.

O loving heart of Jesus, it is now up to you to make wholly yours this poor heart which in the past was so unthankful and, through its own fault, empty of your love. Inflame this heart with your love, as your heart is burning with love for me.

Make my will be wholly united with your will so that I shall not will anything not willed by you. From now on your holy will shall be the rule for all my actions, all my thoughts, all my desires. Lord, I trust that you do not deny me the grace to live up to this resolution which I make today at your feet, to embrace with peace whatever you dispose for me and for all that I have in my life and in my death".

(Prayer of St Alphonsus)

19

Learning to love in the Heart of Jesus

> "Dwell in me as I in you. No branch can bear fruit by itself, but only if it remains united with the vine; no more can you bear fruit, unless you remain united with me. I am the vine, and you the branches. He who dwells in me, as I dwell in him, bears much fruit; for apart from me you can do nothing. He who does not dwell in me is thrown away like a withered branch. The withered branches are heaped together, thrown on the fire, and burnt. If you dwell in me, and my words dwell in you, ask what you will, and you shall have it. This is my Father's glory, that you may bear fruit in plenty and so be my disciples. As the Father has loved me, so I have loved you. Dwell in my love. If you heed my commands you will dwell in my love, as I have heeded my Father's commands and dwell in his love. I have spoken thus to you, so that my love may be in you, and your joy complete. This is my commandment: love one another, as I have loved you" (Jn 15:4–12).

THE tender love of Jesus is most personal. It touches everyone in his inmost being, in his heart. Yet it may not be privatized. It is an all-embracing rallying call. Jesus wants his disciples to learn not only to love him but also to love, with him, all whom he loves and to love them, as it were, with his own loving heart.

Therefore, it is now time to concentrate on a feature of the devotion to the Sacred Heart which has been mentioned time and time again: learning to be so much at home in the heart of Jesus that we join him willingly and joyously in his love for all whom his powerful love has created and redeemed.

First in the priority of values is learning to love Jesus, to enter fully into the mystery of his loving heart by loving him in return. This is expressed in the fundamental command: "Dwell in me". But immediately and unavoidably follows the call from the Father to love, with Jesus, his glory and his glorious command, "Love one another!" This means joining Jesus and the Father in their liberating, redeeming and healing love for all humankind. Pius XII applies this to the essence of the devotion to the Sacred Heart: "Thus we reach easily the conclusion that the veneration of the most sacred heart of Jesus is essentially the cult of love by which God, in Jesus, has loved us and, at the same time, the exercise of our love for God and love for the rest of humankind".

To allow Jesus to conquer our hearts means to enter into a stream of love. It implies that we "discard the old selfish nature and put on the new nature which is constantly renewed in the image of its creator and brought to know God". The imperative of grace follows: "Then put on the garments that suit God's chosen people, his own, his beloved: compassion, kindness, humility, gentleness, patience. Be forbearing with one another, and forgiving, where any of you has cause for complaint; you must forgive as the Lord forgave you. To crown all, there must be love, to bind all together and complete the whole. Let Christ's peace be arbiter in your hearts; to this peace you were called as members of a single body. And be filled with gratitude" (Col 3:12–15).

St Therese of Lisieux grasped the essence of the devotion to the Heart of Jesus by her great desire to find her place and role in the mystical body by being a loving person in the very heart of Jesus. It is well known that she would have liked to see women ordained priests and to become one of them. But this desire did not upset her, for she found a most appropriate answer: that more important than all the ministries and charisms in the mystical body is to be immersed wholly in the radiation and circulation of love that comes from the heart of Jesus and unites us with his loving heart. This should be the decisive desire of every priest, religious and layperson.

We proclaim the love of Jesus trustworthily and understandably by loving his own as he did. "His own" are his friends, the believers, the loving. Those who offend, insult, hate and persecute his friends drive a lance into the heart of Jesus more cruelly than the soldier who opened his heart with the lance after his death. Saul had to experience this when Jesus threw him from horseback on the road to Damascus and asked him, "Saul, Saul, why do you persecute me?" (Acts 9:4).

But the love of Jesus reaches beyond those who are his own. He has come to save sinners. He celebrates the messianic meal with tax collectors and persons of ill-repute. While still on the cross, before his heart was broken, he prayed for those who had crucified him, for all his enemies. Hence our devotion to the Sacred Heart becomes serious and truthful when we learn from Jesus to pardon with healing love and to love the unloving and the unloved.

Jesus came to save the world from the killing frost of lovelessness. With gentle love he meets the unloved and the despised and makes them able to receive and reciprocate love. For those who have a true devotion to the Sacred Heart there are no "hopeless cases"; they don't write off anyone.

That Jesus' love for us is "costly" is confirmed by his most bitter suffering and the shedding of his precious blood. We cannot effectively enter into the redeeming stream of his love for people without being conformed to his sacrificial love, without being ready to suffer for love's sake. Pius XI suggests, as a practical example of this "sacrificial love", a simple life-style in constant readiness to assist the poor and the unloved.

It is a lifelong task to learn how to love Jesus and to enter into the redeeming stream of his love for all. Nobody should dream that he or she has already met thc mark. Whoever is thoroughly captured by Jesus' love will, like the Apostle, "press on, hoping to take hold of that for which Christ once took hold of me. . . forgetting what is behind me, and reaching out for that which lies ahead" (Phil 3 : 12–13).

Knowing Christ lovingly and lovingly striving for a better knowledge of him go hand in hand with a greater love of neighbour and a clearer discernment for the kind of love that can be offered in the name of Jesus. Friends of the heart of Jesus strive for the kind of love of neighbour which Christ can somehow recognize as his own.

* * *

O most loving Heart of Jesus, what a fool I was when I concentrated all my energies on amassing all kinds of knowledge and skills, while I strove with only a divided heart for the real

G

wisdom of knowing you and your way of loving people! I am afraid that I must simply confess that in this supreme art I have always remained inept. Yet, thanks to your grace, my heart is still able to sense the folly and perversion of proportions. I am deeply grieved by this, and in this sorrow I see a sign of your gracious patience and forgiveness. So, with your grace I dare to hope that from now on I shall seek first the reign of your love and all else for your sake.

Yet, because I am rightly afraid of my inconsistency, superficiality and weakness, I implore you, by your loving heart, to confirm my resolution, increase my desire to seek first your love and the art of loving people in union with your heart, whatever the price may be.

Open to me the meaning of Holy Scripture so that, like the hearts of the disciples on the road to Emmaus, mine too may burn with love for you and with you. Pour out on all of us your Holy Spirit so that we may become a credible community of disciples, and the world may believe that the reign of love is at hand.

20

"Uno corde" — Concord of Christ's disciples

> "The whole body of believers was united in heart and soul" (Acts 4:32).
>
> "It is not for these alone that I pray, but for those also who through their words put their faith in me; may they all be one: as thou, Father, art in me and I in thee, so also may they be in us, that the world may believe that thou didst send me. The glory which thou gavest me I have given to them, that they may be one, as we are one; I in them and thou in me, may they be perfectly one. Then the world will learn that thou didst send me, that thou didst love them as thou didst me" (Jn 17:20–23).

UNITY, solidarity, peace, as they come from God and lead to him, are not first a matter of organization but of the heart: of the inmost being of persons who are able and willing to build bridges among people and, by healthy relationships, can contribute also to the healing of public life.

It is not written that in the apostolic community in Jerusalem all had the same ideas or that they agreed on all problems. On the contrary, the Acts of the Apostles tell us that there was partial disagreement on important questions. But they were "united in heart and soul". They met each other in the tender and strong love of Jesus, knowing that Jesus loved them all and called them all to share in his redeeming, all-inclusive love. They knew that they were sent for a redemptive witness which could not exist without their being united in heart and soul.

This unity in heart was fruitful and led to radical approaches for community life: no one should suffer misery while others had more than enough; there should be spontaneous and generous sharing; the poor and widows coming from different cultures should be honoured and helped without discrimination. They sought the best possible organizational solutions through respectful dialogue. Everything flowed from their deeply-felt solidarity.

John's gospel leads us to the unfathomable mystery from which such splendid unity of heart and soul arose. The disciples knew themselves to be inserted into the supreme mystery of the loving unity between Father and Son. Jesus loves us with the same love as the Father loves us. The Father's love for Jesus is inseparably united with his love for us. In the same way, the love between you and me cannot be severed from the covenanted love of Jesus for his Church, indeed, for the whole of humanity, according to the mandate of the Father.

This ineffable mystery marks all of our christian life. We are entitled to join Jesus who calls almighty God "Abba — dear Father", but in the form, "our Father", thus reminding us that this wonderful prerogative is based on saving solidarity in Christ. We honour the way in which God glorifies his name when we join him and Jesus in an all-embracing unity and love, in mutual respect and concord.

Without sincere effort towards unity in heart and mind we can neither hallow the name of the Father nor greet the coming of his kingdom, for we are not yet conformed to his loving will. The Father's will is clearly described for us in the farewell discourses and the great prayer of Jesus (Jn 13 : 17): "that they may be perfectly one, as we are one". Therefore, in the prayer taught by Jesus himself and in our life, concord has high priority.

Unity in heart and mind among adorers of the Sacred Heart of Jesus is not an imperative imposed from outside but a stream of living water arising from within those who believe and have opened themselves to the Spirit sent by Jesus. It is the expression of our vital insertion into the life of Christ. "Let your bearing towards one another arise out of your life in Christ Jesus" (Phil 2 : 5). This is the main perspective and foundation of the counsel imparted to us by the Apostle: "If then our common life in Christ yields anything to stir the heart, any loving consolation, any sharing of the Spirit, any warmth of affection or compassion, fill up my cup of happiness by thinking and feeling alike, with the same love for one another, the same turn of mind, and a common care for unity" (Phil 2 : 1–2).

In his letter to the Ephesians, Paul's appeal for concord and unity in heart and mind is grounded on the basic truths of our faith. "Be humble always and gentle, and patient too. Be forbearing with one another and charitable. Spare no effort to make fast with bonds of peace the unity which the Spirit gives. There is *one* body and *one* Spirit, as there is also *one* hope held out in God's call to you: *one* Lord, *one* faith, *one* baptism; *one* God and Father of all, who is over all and through all and in all" (Eph 4:2–6).

In this same light we see the various charisms and ministries for the building up of the mystical body of Christ (Eph 4:7–16). "Bonded and knit together by every constituent joint, the whole frame grows through the due activity of each part, and builds itself up in love" (Eph 4:16). We find the same emphasis and motivation in the first letter to the Corinthians. All depends on that love which conforms and unites us to Christ and thus among ourselves. "Put love first" (1 Cor 14:1).

*   *   *

Lord Jesus, most loving and most worthy of love, we thank you that, through the gospel of John to whom you have given the sharp eye of an eagle for the mysteries of your heart, you share with us your prayer for unity in heart and mind, so that we might live united with your heart and thus glorify the Father. O most gracious heart of our Redeemer, you have suffered terribly from seeing discord among your disciples, their ridiculous rivalry, their jealousy and envy for higher positions. And what must your sensitive heart have suffered when faced with our sloth in matters of mutual love and concord, and with our laziness in dedicating ourselves to the art of concord in heart and mind and learning to love each other as you love us? Forgive us for failing to pray zealously for this grace and art, when you have desired so much to grant it to those who pray to you sincerely and unceasingly.

Lord, open our eyes and our hearts and make us clearsighted for what is essential. Strengthen our resolution to pray, to act and, when there is need, to suffer for the great cause of unity of your followers.

21

The symbol of the Good Shepherd

> "I am the good shepherd; the good shepherd lays down his life for his sheep. The hireling, when he sees the wolf coming, abandons the sheep and runs away, because he is no shepherd and the sheep are not his. Then the wolf harries the flock and scatters the sheep. The man runs away because he is a hireling and cares nothing for the sheep.
>
> I am the good shepherd; I know my own sheep and my sheep know me — as the Father knows me and I know the Father — and I lay down my life for the sheep. But there are other sheep of mine, not belonging to this fold, whom I must bring in; and they too will listen to my voice. There will then be one flock, one shepherd. The Father loves me because I lay down my life, to receive it back again" (Jn 10: 11–17).

THE symbol of the good shepherd and Jesus' testimony to it found an echo in a culture of shepherds similar to that of the later symbol of the "heart". In the symbol of the good shepherd it is really the heart of Jesus speaking. He tells of a kind of mutual knowing between the good shepherd and his sheep, between him and his disciples, which he compares with the loving knowledge between himself and the heavenly Father. It is a knowledge of the heart. The self-giving love of which he speaks is the same love of which the pierced heart of Jesus on the cross speaks to us forever.

In this same symbolism of the good shepherd and with the same emphasis as in his heart-revealing prayer at the Last Supper, Jesus speaks on the unity and concord of the redeemed. Both the symbolism of the shepherd and the reality of the loving heart of Jesus, forever beating for us, inspire apostolic zeal and dedication to the cause of peace and unity in all genuine disciples of Christ.

Hesychius describes this point well when he writes: "The

apostles are the heart of Jesus, organs of his love". Those who "dwell in Jesus' heart", conformed with his redeeming love — the present-day apostles — will show a burning zeal for the salvation of all. Knowing the heart and mind of the Good Shepherd and loving with his heart, they can help others to discover their own inner strengths and thereby hear the voice and understand the love of the Redeemer.

After his resurrection Jesus, the Good Shepherd, challenges Peter three times about his love. Following Peter's humble, stumbling assurance of his love, Jesus, in gracious confirmation of Peter's supreme office as good shepherd, made the tripled appeal: "Then, tend my lambs, tend my sheep, feed my sheep". Here, Peter is the prototype. All apostolates, all pastoral activity can be fruitful and truthful only when they arise from humble and loving hearts.

Paul expresses this truth in a way that directly reminds us of Jesus' tender love for the redeemed. "God knows how I am loving you in the heart of Christ Jesus himself" (Phil 1:8). A good translation reads: "loving you as Christ Jesus loves you".

It is simply impossible to enter intimately into the love of the Redeemer without being seized by his zeal for the salvation of all. This experience of being irresistibly attracted by the passionate love of Jesus for all, especially for sinners and those who do not yet know him, has been and still is the basis of many priestly and religious vocations. I am convinced that we need a strong revival of the devotion to the Heart of our Redeemer to overcome the present crisis of priestly vocations.

But we should think not only of the apostolate in the ministerial priesthood. It is the vocation of all believers to be an active part of the Church which is an apostolic community. Every Christian whose heart is captured by the redeeming love of Jesus will be an apostle in his or her own place of life. The key is always the being enraptured by the loving heart of Jesus, the Good Shepherd. Then we shall bear each other's burdens, encourage and kindly correct one another, and enkindle in many hearts a great enthusiasm for the Divine Redeemer and his ongoing work on earth.

It is an undeniable truth that God knows many ways to lead people to eternal salvation. However, it is a deplorable error to infer from this, as some poorly instructed and superficial

Christians do, that the apostolic zeal and tireless effort to lead people to the knowledge and love of Christ is not particularly important. If one has a profound experience of what it means to "know Jesus", the Good Shepherd, and to be known by him — as the Father knows Jesus and Jesus knows the Father (Jn 10:14) — the bliss of such a loving knowledge will make one yearn, as Paul did, with Christ's own love, to bring as many people as possible to the same knowledge, love and blissful trust in the Good Shepherd.

We cannot really praise God for the full revelation of his love through Jesus, the Good Shepherd, without longing to see God loved and praised by all and to see the joy and peace of those who come to such a saving, liberating knowledge through our cooperation. Jesus, who died for all and is risen for all, considers all people — every man, woman and child — as his own. If he calls us to share in his love and mission as the Good Shepherd who knows his own and wants to lead all into the one flock then nothing can divert us from the wonderful and urgent vocation to make Jesus known and loved.

Faced with the fact that humankind is exposed to the most atrocious threats of violence, exploitation, hatred, manipulation and even nuclear self-destruction, every Christian should realize that humankind needs nothing more urgently than to come to know the saving message of the Good Shepherd who knows how to guide and protect us, if we acknowledge him and entrust ourselves to him.

Why should we not have the courage to warn people into what an abyss they will plunge if they refuse the saving love offered by Jesus Christ and the Father? If we have not this courage and do not feel the urgency to proclaim the gospel and give witness to it for the salvation of humankind, then we should be shocked by the realization that we have not yet allowed Christ to captivate us by his love and to conform us to his heart as Good Shepherd.

It is an historical fact that the increase in the devotion to the Sacred Heart during and after the French Revolution led to great apostolic zeal. The many congregations dedicated in a special way to the Sacred Heart have been outstanding pioneers in missionary incentive and perseverance during the last two centuries.

* * *

Lord Jesus, you are the Good Shepherd, foretold in the Old Testament. You have shown us the meaning of the prophecy: "The Lord Yahweh says this: I am going to look after my flock myself . . . I myself will pasture my sheep, I myself will show them where to rest — it is the Lord Yahweh who speaks. I shall look for the lost ones, bring back the stray, bandage the wounded and make the weak strong. I shall watch over the healthy. I shall be a true shepherd to them" (Ezek 34 : 11–16).

By doing all this you have shown us the Father. Your love knows no bounds. Even if we run away and go hopelessly astray, still you want to find us and heal us. O Good Shepherd, make us grateful for such a great love and loving care. Then gratitude will inspire us to accept generously and joyfully your invitation to share in your mission as good shepherds.

Heart of our Saviour, instill your love into the hearts of all who share in the ministry of shepherds in the Church and in the hearts of those whom you have chosen for this sublime vocation. Teach them by your Spirit how to become a true image of you, so that all may come to realize that, in them and through them, you yourself look after your people and tend them most lovingly.

In the present crisis of priestly vocations we pray to you, as you have told us, to send workers into your vineyard; awaken again, in all of us, the spirit of shepherds who are full of enthusiasm and who radiate joy, peace, kindness and loving care. Give priests the special charism to discover priestly vocations and to inspire apostolic zeal in the hearts of all the faithful, so that all may realize what a great honour and joy it is to participate in your mission as Good Shepherd.

Assist spouses to become for each other a true image of your kind, patient and healing love. Grant to parents the wisdom and strength to raise their children in your love and to join you in the work of salvation.

Lord Jesus, you have spoken exultantly of those believers who "know" you in a way similar to the way you know the Father. We beg you, by your most loving heart, to grant us a sharp sense for the essential, so that we do not desire anything more than to know you lovingly and to grow constantly in this love and knowledge, and thus help each other on the road of salvation.

22

The compassionate heart of the Divine Physician

> "The pharisees and the lawyers of their sect complained to his disciples: 'Why do you eat and drink', they said, 'with tax-collectors and sinners?' Jesus answered them: 'It is not the healthy that need a doctor, but the sick; I have not come to invite virtuous people, but to call sinners to repentance' " (Lk 5:30–32).

> Jesus "went around the whole of Galilee, teaching in the synagogues, preaching the gospel of the kingdom, and curing whatever illness or infirmity there was among the people. His fame reached the whole of Syria; and sufferers from every kind of illness, racked with pain, possessed by devils, epileptic, or paralyzed, were brought to him, and he cured them" (Mt 4:23–25).

WHILE the title "good shepherd" is a symbol of abiding care taken from a specific culture, the name "Divine Physician", by which Jesus was honoured in early christianity, is more than a symbol, just as language about the "heart" of Jesus is more than a symbol. These titles bespeak a deep reality with inexhaustible symbolic riches. Jesus is more a healer than any human physician. He alone can restore full health and wholeness to body and soul. He is also the most compassionate physician already foretold, as such, by the prophet: "Ours were the sufferings he bore, ours the sorrows he carried . . . through his wounds we were healed" (Is 53:4–5).

From beginning to end, the public activity of Jesus is marked by his healing ministry, reaching its peak in his passion. When taken prisoner, as if he were a bandit, he lovingly healed the ear of the high priest's servant wounded by Peter (Lk 22:51). Hanging on his cross he healed the heart and soul of the criminal crucified with him. And this is only the prelude. From the pierced heart of our Redeemer flow forever streams of healing graces. The old germanic word for "saviour" was "Heiland", and it is still much used. It means the one who brings at the same time salvation and healing. He has come to make us whole and holy.

Jesus is the merciful Samaritan who, faced with the poor man fallen into the hands of robbers, is moved with compassion, takes loving care of him and does so at his own expense. We all are included in this parable. In the misery of our sins and with all the sufferings that derive from them, we are met by the most compassionate physician.

Jesus is the healer of those who, with the poisoned lance of their sins, have wounded unto death the healer of sinners. The wound in his heart, which has become glorious in his resurrection, continues to send forth streams of salvation. Our sins have deserved bitter wrath, but Jesus meets us with gentleness, kindness, healing compassion. His heart, pierced by us, remains open for us as a fountain of salvation.

But his healing compassion clearly informs us also that healing implies sincere conversion on our part. How could we be healed if we prefer to be strangers to this loving heart instead of turning to him with grateful love? Jesus cannot but hate sin, since it is an insult against the all-holy Creator and Redeemer. But Jesus looks at the sinner as a poor brother or sister who has foolishly wounded himself or herself and has run into dark exile. He calls the sinner back to hearty friendship and offers him or her a new heart, a loving heart and a grateful memory.

In Christ's mission, proclamation of the good news is inseparable from call to conversion and healing. When Jesus proclaims the gospel of the beatitudes as gift and call, a healing power of love "goes out from him". Jesus praying on the mount is symbol of his absolute union with the Father. This is the source of his healing. But Jesus, being one with the Father, cannot stay aloof on the mount when he sees our misery. He comes down from the height to heal people burdened with guilt and suffering.

This is beautifully expressed by Luke, the physician: "Jesus came down the hill with the disciples and took his stand on the level ground. There was a great concourse of his disciples and great numbers of people from Jerusalem and Judea and from the seaboard of Tyre and Sidon, who had come to listen to him, and to be cured of their diseases. Those who were troubled with unclean spirits were cured; and everyone in the crowd was trying to touch him, because power went out from him and cured them all" (Lk 6:17–19).

If we are yearning to be freed from evil spirits, such as self-righteousness, idolatry of status or money, hardness of heart, and to be cured of our moral and other diseases, then we must equally yearn to listen to Jesus and to let the good news enter our hearts. He who floods us with his healing love in the beatitudes shows us also the way to heal hearts, to heal human relationships and to heal public life.

An absolute condition for being healed and becoming true sharers in Jesus' healing ministry is to conform ourselves to his compassionate love. "How blest are those who show mercy; mercy shall be shown to them" (Mt 5:7). Jesus teaches us by word and example what true mercy and compassion mean. "Learn what that text means, 'I require mercy, not sacrifice!' I did not come to invite virtuous people, but sinners" (Mt 9:13).

In the context the expression, "virtuous people", means those who meticulously observe certain details of their interpretation of law while looking down on others with a hardened heart. They are not longing for healing; indeed, they stubbornly turn away from God's healing mercy. They offer vain sacrifices and refuse the real sacrifice of overcoming their arrogance and renouncing everything that blocks compassionate healing.

By his own compassion and merciful actions Jesus turns our hearts to the heavenly Father: "Be compassionate as your Father is compassionate" (Lk 6:36). With Paul, who has wonderfully experienced God's mercy, we all are to "praise the God and Father of our Lord Jesus Christ, the all-merciful Father, the God whose consolation never fails!" (2 Cor 1:3).

If our heart is beating somehow in consonance with Jesus' heart, then not only will we forgive our adversaries from the depth of our heart but will also try to meet them in healing love. This heals our hurt memory and sentiments, too. However, if we are truly inserted into the compassionate healing ministry of Jesus, we do not concentrate much on our own needs but more directly on the needs of others to be healed from hatred and other "evil spirits". This, of course, does not mean that in this process we should not be concerned also for our own integrity, which is a basic good for us and for the mystical body of Christ.

Paul gives us an attractive picture of redeemed and redeeming love when he says, "Love is patient, love is kind and envies no one . . . not quick to take offence. Love keeps no score of wrongs" (1 Cor 13 : 4–6). It should be noted that Paul does not say, "love *must*". Love, flowing from the heart of Jesus and from the heart of the disciple transformed by intimate friendship with Jesus and by the power of the Spirit, *is* compassionate, *is* patient. Compassionate and healing thoughts, words and deeds flow from within those believers who drink thirstily from the fountain of salvation (cf. Jn 7 : 37–39). What is decisive, therefore, is that we turn to Jesus with heart and mind: that we "dwell in Christ Jesus".

Those who are touched by the compassionate love of the Redeemer realize from within what is the meaning of: "If you are helping others in distress, do it cheerfully" and "give with all your heart" (Rom 12 : 8).

Whoever has learned mercy from the loving heart of Jesus has learned also a new understanding of God's saving justice. Such a person will no longer be anguished about his own selfish advantage or points of honour, but will hunger and thirst that God's saving justice may prevail (cf. Mt 5 : 6).

The encyclical *Dives in Misericordia* (Rich in Mercy), of John Paul II is not only a major contribution to a right understanding of the Sacred Heart of Jesus but also an important part of Catholic social doctrine. Those who have learned to praise the God and Father of our Lord Jesus Christ for his compassion and saving justice will commit themselves to work for the solution of threatening conflicts as a matter of justice but also as a matter of compassion. Their compassion will be for the poor, on the one hand, but not less for those hard-minded rich who are the most miserable on earth. Faced with such contrasts as that between super-affluent societies and the hundreds of millions who die of starvation, they themselves will fall into all kinds of perversion and trouble, if they are not converted to justice and mercy.

Jesus' mercy extends to all dimensions of human life, the misery of sinfulness, illness of body and mind, extreme poverty, oppression, social disorder. "When Jesus came ashore, he saw a great crowd; and his heart went out to them, because they were like sheep without a shepherd; and he had much to teach them" (Mk 6:34). Surely people need the good news above all, but the gospel does not stop there. It keeps referring to Jesus' teaching. It tells us that Jesus also took care that his listeners had something to eat.

With the magisterium of the Church, I steadfastly reject the approach of those who think that liberation and redemption happen mainly or even exclusively through structural changes by economic and political revolution. The first requirement is and remains the "revolution of being", the healing of hearts and minds, and faith in the resurrection. This does not at all invalidate the acute relevance of healing public life through good political planning, good leaders, and by our competent participation in shaping beneficial public opinion regarding economic and social conditions.

If, in their innermost being, Christians are conformed to the compassion of Jesus and his hunger and thirst for saving justice to prevail, then there will also be a growth of the best vocations for healing public life, including politics at all levels.

* * *

O Heart of our Redeemer, you have shown us the Father in his compassion and saving justice. Your heart goes out to all who are in need. We hope to praise your mercy and with you the mercy of the heavenly Father for all eternity. Help us in our commitment to mercy and saving justice in this valley of tears. Let it be the fitting prelude to this praise.

Lord Jesus, we live in a world with many hardened hearts and threatening conflicts. Contamination constantly tempts us; and we cannot deny that we are already partially contaminated. Lord, heal us, and make us effective signs of your healing mercy and justice.

Divine Saviour, send into this world, ensnared in alienation, men and women who will credibly bring into it the gospel of mercy and peace.

Heart of Jesus, touch affluent nations, the wealthy, groups and individuals, with a ray of your compassionate love and your zeal for saving justice, so that they may learn what kind of justice you and your heavenly Father want from them.

O meek and powerful Heart, you can heal our hearts from coldness and sloth and make us a blessing for many people by our deep repentance and conversion. Lord, let this happen soon!

23

Jesus, humble of heart, make us humble

> "When that day comes I will remove your proud boasters from your midst; and you will cease to strut on my holy mountain. In your midst I will leave a humble and lowly people, and those who are left in Israel will seek refuge in the name of Yahweh" (Zeph 3:11–12).
>
> "At that favoured time Jesus spoke these words: 'I thank thee, Father, Lord of heaven and earth, for hiding these things from the learned and wise, and revealing them to the simple. Yes, Father, such was thy choice'. Everything is entrusted to me by my Father; and no one knows the Son but the Father, and no one knows the Father but the Son and those to whom the Son may choose to reveal him. Come to me, all whose work is hard, whose load is heavy; and I will give you relief. Bend your necks to my yoke, and learn from me, for I am gentle and humble-hearted; and your hearts will find relief" (Mt 11:25–29).

PRIDE and arrogance tie up human hearts and destroy bridges between people. Indeed, they tend to undermine all saving bridges. Pride is the incendiary bomb that destroys hearts and the earth. It is the final cause of the icy devastation of lovelessness and injustice.

Our humble-hearted Saviour guides us in the healing of wounded hearts, of painful memories, of alienated relationships and difficult human conditions. He builds bridges whereby heart finds heart.

The Eternal Word of the Father chose the path of humility in becoming one-of-us. He did not come in earthly power and glory but, under the sign of the most humble mother, was born in the misery of a stable. "He who can do great things suffers hunger and thirst; he is exhausted. He is made captive, is beaten, crucified and murdered. This is the road: walk in humility and you will inherit eternity" (St Augustine).

Jesus washes his disciples' feet, knowing well how much they and we need such an example.

Even the glorified Lord continues to be the great sign of saving humility in the sacraments of faith. He speaks to our hearts and performs his miracles of grace through the weak, earthly signs of the sacraments. Hidden under the sacramental figures, his almighty love is near to us. In them he continues his encounter with us until the final revelation of his glory.

What astounding, yet sublime love! Almighty God reveals himself in the most abject humility, beginning with his incarnation and unto the ignominy of the cross. "The divine nature was his from the first" (Phil 2:6), yet he makes himself the servant of all. In Jesus' humility, almighty God has shown us the absolute boundlessness of the power of his love.

But one thing remains forever intolerable: God cannot accept vainglory and arrogance in creatures. "The arrogant heart and mind he has put to rout, but the humble have been lifted high" (Lk 1:51–22).

In his prayer of self-revelation as Son, Jesus praises the Father for revealing himself to the humble-hearted. In his true humanity Jesus is the embodiment of the humble. "No one knows the Father but the Son", and the Son cannot but choose the same road. The humble-hearted will know him and, through him, the Father. Only the humble let God be God in all their life.

Only if we affirm Jesus as the Servant-Messiah can we be healed from the deadly plague of vanity. Otherwise we are unable to share in Christ's loving knowledge of the Father.

For many people God seems to be unreal, far away; he seems to be silent and hiding himself. Often one of the reasons is the person's pride which, centering on himself, keeps him aloof. He becomes enemy to his fellowmen and an unbearable burden to himself.

Jesus calls us; he reaches out to us in our alienation and self-made exile. "Come to me!" In his compassion he yearns to free us from the plagues and the blindness which reflect the pride of the world and our own pride. To "bend our necks under his yoke" means a faithful "yes" to his humble-heartedness, which is an essential dimension of his being and his mission. His humility is the road which divine love takes from celestial glory to our lowliness. It is Jesus' way to our hearts and the astonishing revelation of his heart. It is also the signpost for our journey on the road to redemption and to everlasting life with God

By his humility the Redeemer shows us how to find rest for our hearts and how to become a source of peace, kindness and heartfelt compassion for many people. The decisive beginning of the learning process is an awed thankfulness and praise for this amazing way of the Son of God made son-of-man, the One-of-us. Our second step is profound shame for our vanity. Amazement and gratitude prepare a wholesome contrition as well as a feeling of relief and a renewed trust.

For believers a basic requirement is to find the courage to learn from Jesus the supreme art of loving humility and humble love, whatever the cost.

Humility comes to Christ's disciples not as a kind of imposition but as a liberation. Christlike love *is* humble; we learn this from the heart of Jesus. Therefore, it is evident that we can learn gentleness and humility not apart from love but only as a substantial dimension of love. The more we love Jesus, the more his secret of humility becomes accessible to us; and the more eagerly we learn humility and gentleness, the more Jesus can reveal to us the mysteries of his heart. He can show us the Father and teach us adoration in spirit and truth.

Gradually, then, we find peace for our souls and experience ever more the blessings of humility for ourselves and for others.

In today's world this is foreign language. But it is mother-tongue in the kingdom of Christ. Happy are those who dare to hear it, to learn it, to speak it and to give thanks with it and for it.

* * *

My dear Lord and Saviour, I come to you burdened and oppressed by many worries and slavish work, by an unbearable yoke which I have imposed on myself because of my lack of humility. It is a burden which I have deserved, but it is also the heavy yoke of a sinful world, of collective pride and arrogance. We are tied together in this lamentable condition. I groan and sigh, realizing my plight in this double slavery of mine and of the world. What a relief if I listen to your invitation, "Come to me all whose load is heavy!" Yes, now I dare to come.

The more I meditate on the crushing burdens you have carried in your humility, accepting even the most atrocious humiliation from proud and arrogant human beings, the more I am filled with grateful wonder. In your divine glory and your human humility you are totally Other, so different from the close-minded and high-handed adamic man. You *are* the wholly Other, the only true God, so unlike man-made gods. You have come into the valley of tears where misery is constantly multiplied by humankind's ridiculous pride. You come with the astonishing remedy, the humility of the Son of God, of the Redeemer, who has freely made himself "one-of-us" in all things except sin: the totally holy and humble One.

You come to us whose vanity and pride are odious. You come on the royal road of humility, showing us that this is the way to you and to the heart of the Father, the way to the hearts of our fellowmen and the way of salvation.

Humble heart of our Divine Master, I entrust myself to your school. I want to learn from you, day by day, the royal way of humility. It is our own love that teaches us.

Lord, transform our hearts, make them mirror-images of your own heart. Make them fountains of healing for many. Lord, make us humble.

24

Love's victory

"What can separate us from the love of Christ? Can affliction or hardship? Can persecution, hunger, nakedness, peril or the sword? 'We are being done to death for thy sake all day long', as Scripture says; 'we have been treated like sheep for slaughter' — and yet, in spite of all, overwhelming victory is ours through him who loved us. For I am convinced that there is nothing in death or life, in the realm of spirits or superhuman powers, in the world as it is or the world as it shall be, in the forces of the universe, in heights or depths — nothing in all creation that can separate us from the love of God in Christ Jesus our Lord" (Rom 8:35–39).

LOVE is the only absolute power in heaven and on earth. For God is Love, and his salvation plan for the world is wholly a design of love. But salvation becomes effective only where man gratefully receives and responds to the divine love. This totally free gift of God cannot be forced upon any person.

Praised be God, love found its most perfect dwelling place on earth in the heart of the God-Man, Jesus Christ. The Word of God became flesh to bring us the love from above and, in the name of humankind, to give the response of perfect love. Jesus came to win us over to its salvific cause. Though wounded and tempted by all the lovelessness and hatred in the human race, the heart of Jesus has proved itself victorious against all assaults, and has brought home to the Father humankind's thankful love.

To his last heart-beat Jesus fought for the victory of love. The most violent resistance of this sinful world against liberating love had to contribute to make love's triumph on the Saviour's cross even more glorious and evident. Crucified, Jesus prays for his torturers and slanderers. Humiliated by the malicious plan to crucify him with two common criminals, he makes one of them the first to be brought home by him to the eternal celebration of the victory of love.

The group of the faithful who stood under Jesus' cross was, indeed, painfully small. But in Mary, his mother, the new Eve, in the compassionate women and the loving John, there was the first visible design of the new family of Jesus, believers in the triumph of love. They saw Jesus' heart, pierced by the soldier's lance, flooding the sinful world with the saving bath of water and blood. And after Jesus' resurrection they were privileged to see the glory of his opened heart. Thomas was even allowed to touch it with his hand. For him and for all believers this heart is the great sign of God's victory and the sure promise of final conquest.

Faith tells us that love is triumphant in the total gift of self. The redeemed find their true selves when they leave behind their selfish selves in the total service of love.

While Jesus was reaching the most abject point of humiliation and disdain he was already exalted in and for the victory of his all-embracing love. He had begun to draw to his heart all those whom the Father had given him.

The firm and faithful hope for love's final conquest belongs to the very substance of christianity. It is not worthwhile to dedicate one's life to any cause inferior to that of love, or to work hard for anything that is not inspired by redeeming love and does not serve its cause. But the cause of love for which Christ came is, indeed, worth all dedication and even all suffering. This is the one precious pearl that is worth more than everything else. The reward for those who have given everything away for love's sake is now the down-payment on nothing less than love itself, the abode of love for all eternity.

This victorious love is not our invention or our achievement. It is thoroughly grace, an undeserved gift flowing from the heart of the Redeemer. But love looks for grateful hearts ready to enrich the hearts of others.

There is nothing we can pray for with greater confidence than for this love. The heart of Jesus is the certain assurance that he himself is longing to bestow on us this best-of-all of his gifts. We ask for it in humble and persevering prayer, for we can receive it only if we recognize God as God, the source and goal of all love, and recognize also how much we need this absolutely underserved gift. Praying for this love which conquers all, we meet the inmost longing of the heart of Jesus and, indeed, of the heavenly Father to pour out on all believers this precious gift.

As children of Adam and products of a cramped world, we are narrow-minded and locked into our selfish selves. But newborn by grace, and putting all our trust in God, we can say with the Apostle: "I have strength for anything through him who gives me power" (Phil 4:13). To pray for "everything" and for the "strength for anything" is to pray for the supreme and all-embracing gift of redeeming love, for perseverance in learning this noblest art, and for our share in the final victory of love.

If love does not take first place in our prayers and endeavours, then we struggle in vain in the warfare between vices and virtues. But if our hearts are yearning for this water of life, then not even our weaknesses can frighten us. It is good for us to become ever more conscious that we are only "pots of earthenware to contain this treasure", and that "such transcendent power does not come from us, but is God's alone" (1 Cor 4:7).

The final victory of love is especially foreshadowed for us if we love those who are unloved, those who offend or despise us, and if we sow love where hatred hits us, and win others to the reign of love visible in the heart of Jesus.

This victory, including the conquest of our deeply-rooted selfishness and entanglement in collective selfishness, is the victory of faith bearing fruit in love. The greatest work of God, in and through those who expect everything from him, is love. "Everything" means nothing less than unending participation in love's victory.

* * *

Most loving Master, your heart is the trophy of history's greatest triumph. The surge of hatred is dashed by your love. All who refuse your love are like chaff blown away by the wind; and yet you do not even write them off. As long as they live, you will seek them and invite them to the banquet celebrating your love for them.

O Divine Heart filled with love, you have won my heart. You

have widened it, enlivened and enriched it with your most powerful gift, your gracious and attractive love. To you I entrust myself.

The world wants to entice me with dreams of success, achievements and other vain victories. Help me to be vigilant in the fight against these seductions. Grant me wisdom, so that I may have only one thing in mind: the victory of your love in my heart, in my conduct and in the world around me.

It is good that painfully I had to experience my weakness, for now nothing remains for me but to put all my trust in you. If I realize and fully acknowledge that I can do nothing in the realm of saving love but long for it with all my heart and pray for it, then I may not doubt that I shall be admitted to the triumphal procession of those who eternally celebrate with you the victory of your love in us.

My Saviour, humankind needs love; everyone's heart is made for abiding love. We need witnesses of your saving love whose hearts have become fountains of its "living water". Lord, help us to become ever more "light to the world", increase in us faith in your love and trust in its final victory.

25

Love that sets us free

> "Turning to the Jews who had believed in him, Jesus said, 'If you dwell within the revelation I have brought, you are indeed my disciples; you shall know the truth, and the truth will set you free'. They replied, 'We are Abraham's descendants; we have never been in slavery to any man. What do you mean by saying, 'You will become free men'? 'In very truth I tell you', said Jesus, 'that everyone who commits sin is a slave. The slave has no permanent standing in the household, but the son belongs to it forever. If then the Son sets you free, you will indeed be free' " (Jn 8:31–36).

IN one of her letters St Margaret Mary Alacoque describes the devotion to the Sacred Heart as response to "the desire of the heart of Jesus to tear all men away from the reign of Satan and to bring them home into the sweet freedom of the reign of his love". This expresses accurately what Jesus says in the eighth chapter of John's gospel.

Two great questions that move all thinking people today are: "What is truth?" and "What is true freedom?" The two are inseparable. Jesus came to reveal by his being, his actions, his word and finally by his death and resurrection, the saving and liberating truth. In a wholly new way he has restored to humankind the original gift of freedom. The renewed freedom of the redeemed receives its meaning and strength from the love of Christ.

Probably the oldest christian hymn known to us — Phil 2:6–11 — is a liturgical praise of the amazing liberty of the Son of God who in divine freedom "made himself nothing, assuming the nature of a slave". The hymn points to Christ's resurrection which finally makes manifest that unique freedom and the dynamics of love. "Therefore God raised him to the heights and bestowed on him the name above all names".

So we learn from Jesus' heart what true freedom is and what it is not.

Proud man arrogates freedom as his own capital which should pay interest to him alone. He intends to extend his freedom in rebellion against the One who has entrusted it to him. But stolen, arrogated freedom proves false; a road into a self-made slavery with no exit.

How different is the freedom of Jesus! He sees himself and his freedom as gifts from the Father, and in gratitude he freely gives himself back in purest love and loving service. His freedom in being one-with-the-Father proves to be the source of boundless freedom to love us poor sinners with divine and human love. By our sinfulness we are the unloved and unloving, but thanks to the absolute freedom of Christ we know that we are loved. By the power of his Spirit we can share in his love for the Father and for our brethren.

The selfgiving love of Jesus is the great historical event of liberation. In his full humanity Jesus "fulfils" the new law of liberty, the perfect law of love, by the power of the Holy Spirit. By the same power he enables believers to live on the same level of freedom. Paul describes dramatically the difference. The unredeemed experiences himself as "a prisoner under the law" that is in his "bodily members". He is a person "under the law of sin", a slave of his own sinfulness and the world's sin-solidarity. This poor sinner can only cry out, "Miserable creature that I am, who is there to rescue me out of this body doomed to death?" (Rom 7 : 24). But the response of the redeemed, who knows that he was a "slave to the law of sin" because of his selfish self, can be only never-ending praise of God who alone has set us free, "through our Lord Jesus Christ! Thanks be to God" (Rom 7 : 25).

This freedom is not an empty concept or an unattainable ideal. It is a new life 'because in Christ Jesus the life-giving law of the Spirit has set you free from the law of sin and death" (Rom 8 : 2). With the new life comes a new outlook. "Those who live on the level of the Spirit have the spiritual outlook, and that is life and peace" (Rom 8 : 6).

People, who are enticed by the lures of their selfish selves, live in constant contradiction to their true selves as intended by the creator. They live in enmity with their fellowmen, a curse to themselves and to others whom they try to lead into the same slavery and the same perverted outlook on "freedom".

Paul describes the freedom of the children of God in few but immensely rich words: "Everything belongs to you, yet you belong to Christ, and Christ to God" (1 Cor 3:22–23). If we entrust ourselves to Christ as he has entrusted himself to the Father, we are at home in his loving heart. We share his liberating outlook. We are free for each other and can enjoy all the gifts of God as signs of his love, designed to become also signs of mutual love. To live on this level is what the Old Testament prophets foretold under the symbol of "a new heart".

If we follow Christ in that freedom by which he has entrusted himself to his Father in the service of all — thus glorifying the name of the Father — then we shall be free from anguished slavery. We learn to serve God out of grateful love and not out of fear of punishment. "God is love; he who dwells in love is dwelling in God, and God in him. This is for us the perfection of love, to have confidence on the day of judgment, and this we can have, because even in this world we are as he is. There is no room for fear in love; perfect love banishes fear" (1 Jn 4:16–18).

Many people in today's world are so concerned for selfish freedom that they refuse any bond of faithfulness. Of course, they want to talk of love, but only of a love "free" to be unstable. Christ has been faithful unto death and thus has called us into the new and eternal covenant of faithful love. The person who has found life and abode in Jesus is free for a wholehearted "Yes, here I am, call me!" Having put our trust in the Faithful One, we implore and receive the gift of faithful love and courageous responsibility in the service of love. In this way we can set out in a saving solidarity on the road to the eternal kingdom of freedom.

Jesus' freedom is not only a freedom-to-be but the supreme freedom-to-be-for-others, the freedom of the Saviour of the world. If, with Christ, we have conformed our will to God's will, then by grace we can rejoice in the "freedom of the children of God". This is a source of joy for all of creation "because the universe itself is to be freed from the shackles of mortality and enter upon the liberty and splendour of the children of God. Up to the present, we know that the whole created universe groans in all its parts as if in pangs of childbirth" (Rom 8:21–23).

Our growth in solidary freedom is in the interest of the world for which we are meant to be, in Christ and through him, a shining light.

Having entrusted ourselves to Christ we are freed also from fear of death. If we live in Christ "death is gain" (Phil 1:21). The more we find our abode in Jesus' heart, the greater will be our joy when he comes to call us to be with him forever.

The measure of our freedom arises from the measure of our life with Jesus in response to his boundless love and from our joining him in his love for the Father and for the redeemed.

Christian freedom is a light enkindled by the fire of Christ's own love. Inflamed by Jesus' love and inspired by his life we live a life of service to our neighbour and the world.

All of our commitments for outward freedom, for economic, cultural, social and political structures which favour people's freedom, will have effective and lasting results only to the extent that they arise out of our love for Christ.

* * *

Most loving Heart of Jesus, burning hearth of sacrificial love, we praise you and join you in praising the Father for the greatest and all-embracing gift of love. Created by and for your love, O Eternal Word of the Father, we have received superabundant redemption for loving you and loving with you our brothers and sisters in the freedom of adopted children of God. We adore you and the Father, in the Holy Spirit, for your infinite freedom to love us so much.

We, members of sinful humankind, have dishonoured your great gift of freedom, since we did not render thanks for it. In our foolishness we intended to test and demonstrate our own freedom, even in rebellion against your loving will. In this false freedom we left your Father's house to enter into exile and self-made slavery, a slavery for which we become accountable ever anew when we use our freedom against you, the giver of all good gifts. Our greatest punishment and misery are that, as slaves of perverted self-love, we can become unable to love you.

O Word of the Father, breathing the Spirit of love from all eternity, in fulfilment of the saving design of the Father, you shouldered our miseries except the greatest one, the incapacity for true love. Yet our incapacity has made you suffer more than any other human being could suffer, and you have done this out of compassion, in absolute freedom to "bear our burden". We can never marvel enough at your boundless love for us sinners. You meet us with the same freedom with which you met the woman of Samaria, restoring her to dignity and to redeemed love. What more could you have done to bring us home into the freedom of the children of God!

O source of all freedom and love, open our eyes. Let us understand that all talk and endeavour for liberation are in vain, unless we gratefully allow you to make us free for your love. Help us to seek first of all the kingdom of this loving freedom. Thus we pray, O Lord, make us free!

26

The Heart of Jesus and the Paschal Mystery

> "First and foremost, I handed on to you the facts which had been imparted to me: that Christ died for our sins, in accordance with the scriptures; that he was buried; that he was raised to life on the third day, according to the scriptures" (1 Cor 15:3–4).

> "Death is swallowed up; victory is won! O death, where is your victory? O death, where is your sting? The sting of death is sin, and sin gains its power from the law; but, God be praised, he gives us the victory through our Lord Jesus Christ. Therefore, my beloved brothers, stand firm and immovable, and work for the Lord always, work without limit, since you know that your labour cannot be lost" (1 Cor 15:55–58).

THE Pasch-feast (Passover) of the Old Testament has found its fulfilment in the passage of Jesus through the sea of suffering and death, culminating in the victory of the resurrection, the triumph of love. His death is a totally new event, transforming the meaning of death for believers. It becomes "Pasch", the passing-over to the fullness of life.

The mystery of redemption is Christ himself in his passover. In this he is revealed as the One who is "consecrated and sent into the world by the Father" (Jn 10:36). Not only has he wrought redemption; he himself is "our wisdom, and our virtue, and our holiness, and our freedom" (1 Cor 1:30). In his death Jesus is utterly seized and consecrated by the holiness of the heavenly Father. He is the forever-accepted sacrifice, the abiding intercessor for the redeemed. The wound in his heart remains not as a painful laceration but as the open fountain of salvation for all who turn to him.

The death of Jesus is the supreme prayer, adoration in spirit and truth, manifestation of trust and love, sacrifice of praise and intercession. Hence, life in Christ and dying with Christ becomes the christian way of prayer, total openness for the living water flowing from the heart of Jesus.

St Augustine writes: "God wants our yearning to be awakened so that we can receive what he desires to grant us. For God is great, but our capacity to receive is small and miserly. Therefore, we are challenged: 'Widen your hearts!' ".

Jesus' longing to impart to us the riches of his redemption is boundless. His heart is widely opened for us. His death has been the supreme fulfilment of his intercession for us, and its acceptance by the Father is sealed by Christ's resurrection. Thus the heart of the risen and glorious Christ is the abiding assurance that the Father, wanting to lead us through death and resurrection to our final home, urgently invites us to conform ourselves with the prayer of Jesus.

The evangelists inform us that Jesus died at three in the afternoon. In Israel this was the privileged hour of prayer, of the evening sacrifice in the temple. From now on Jesus is the never-ending hour of prayer and the acceptable sacrifice.

This sheds a rich light on what is meant by prayer "in the name of Jesus". We pray truly in his name if we widen our hearts to conform to the will of the Father as Jesus did and if, out of love for God and neighbour, our persevering prayer becomes an all-encompassing yearning for the streams of redemption for all. Believers must find their abode in the heart of Jesus, longing to pray as he prayed, indeed, longing to *become* prayer as he did, in order to pray truly "in the name of Jesus".

His compassionate and interceding love for us continues to such an extent in the risen Lord that he wants to absorb us and make us a part of it. To this end we are consecrated and we consecrate ourselves to the Heart of Jesus so that he can fill us with his redeeming love.

The paschal mystery of the death and resurrection of Christ is the centre and heart of salvation history. Hence, it should be the centre of our own life. The basic dimensions of our being at home in the heart of Jesus and thus in his paschal mystery are:

Grateful remembrance of Jesus' painful passover through the sea of suffering; praise for his having become forever our intercession, "our holiness and freedom", thereby allowing the past to impress on our memory all that the Lord has done for us.

Living in the presence of Jesus here and now, in vigilance and openness to him who has come and comes here and now to prepare us for his final coming and to enable us to be dedicated to his kingdom.

Hope-filled expectation and clear direction on our road to final home-coming in the heart of our Redeemer. Paul describes the life to come as "being at home with the Lord" (2 Cor 5:8). If we, "exiles from the Lord", are so much "at home in the body" that we do not have a great longing for our final abode with the Lord, this is a sign of a still too weak love of God. From the beginning Jesus himself cared about our abiding with him. "Father, I desire that these men, who are thy gift to me, may be with me where I am, so that they may look upon my glory, which thou hast given me before the world began" (Jn 17:24).

In a moving symbol of heartfelt friendship, Scripture entitles us to consider our life in Christ as an invitation to the eternal banquet of love and bliss. We are Jesus' invited guests, "friends of the bridegroom". The celebration of the eucharistic banquet, Holy Communion, and the visit to the Blessed Sacrament remind us of this nearness to Christ, and thus strengthen a grateful memory and vigilant expectation.

If we are living up to our insertion into salvation history with Christ by grateful remembrance of past benefits, vigilant readiness for the present opportunities and responsible foresight for the coming life, then the Lord grants us also the distinctive gifts for this journey for which Christ is both our way and our goal: the gifts of discernment, serenity and, above all, peace and joy in his love.

* * *

My loving Redeemer, most worthy of all my love, I sense a deep longing for a most intimate union with you, yet I know that your desire to see me totally united with you is infinitely greater, since it is the expression of pure love. And while my desire is still marked by inconstancy, your wish to grant me the full experience of your friendship is constant and faithful. Lord, purify and strengthen my longing for total love and dedication to you. Widen my heart! Fill it with your love!

I thank you, Divine Master, for being wholly praise, thanksgiving and intercession in our name. Send forth your Spirit, transform us, help us to be so united with you that we can truthfully pray in your name.

Lord, help me to overcome my superficiality and distraction. Grant me a grateful memory so that I may faithfully meditate on all that you have done and suffered for me. Awaken me from my lethargy and let me no more forget that you have written us into your loving memory.

Lord, help me to be vigilant, ready and able to recognize your coming and your appeal in all events. Give me a sharp eye to find in each hour the most appropriate step towards the final goal.

Fill my heart with great trust in your graciousness, with unbroken hope and serenity in the vicissitudes of our journey and with a wholesome longing to be forever at home with you and the Father in your heavenly kingdom.

Lord, make me one with your passover so that I can look forward to the hour of my death, my passover into our abiding home. Free me from anguish and slavish fear. Grant me the grace of perseverance and a joyous readiness when you come to call me home to you.

27

The Heart of Jesus, source of all joy

> "Yahweh is my strength, my song, he is my salvation. And you will draw water joyfully from the springs of salvation. That day you will say: Give thanks to Yahweh, call his name aloud. Proclaim his deeds to the people, declare his name sublime. Sing of Yahweh, for he has done marvellous things, let them be made known to the world. Cry out for joy and gladness, you dwellers in Zion, for great in your midst is the Holy One of Israel" (Is 12 : 2–6).

THE liturgy of the Sacred Heart of Jesus is, above all, an invitation to joy in the Lord. Jesus wants to see us rejoice in his love. To overlook or minimize this dimension would be to falsify the devotion.

The words of Isaiah 12 : 2 — "You will draw water joyfully" (*Haurietis aquas*) are the first words of the encyclical of Pius XII on the Sacred Heart. The first antiphon of the office of readings is: "In you is the fountain of life; we drink from the streams of your goodness".

If we truly believe in the wholly divine and at the same time wholly human love of Jesus, and in our being invited to the banquet of love and joy in our eternal abode in Jesus' heart, then surely our hearts exult for joy. Then the everyday small troubles will not steal from us our serenity and peace. Indeed, all the sufferings of this time are trifling compared with the love which the Lord has proved for us and the happiness to which he is calling us.

The second reading of the feast, taken from St Bonaventure, is a hymn of joy and an invitation to rejoice: "Run with eager desire to this source of life and light, all you who are vowed to God's service. Come, whoever you may be, and cry out to him with all the strength of your heart: 'O indescribable beauty of the most high and purest radiance of eternal light! Life that gives all life, light that is the source of every other light... Eternal and inaccessible fountain, clear and sweet stream flowing from a hidden spring, unseen by mortal eye! From you flows the river which gladdens the city of God and makes us cry out with joy and thanksgiving, in hymns of praise to you' ".

Lovers find their joy in their mutual love and presence. How much greater must be our joy to know that he, who by nature is love, and has shown us his boundless love, really longs for our love in return. Indeed, he is far more interested in our love than in our deeds. Surely he wants good deeds also, but mainly as sign and fruit of our grateful love.

What is done with love and for love's sake, with the firm assurance that it pleases the beloved one, is done with the ease of enthusiasm. The burden is scarely felt. When good friends meet each other, heart speaks to heart and they find joy in each other. So, too, whoever is seized by the heartfelt love of Jesus turns to him with joy and is happy to thank him and praise him.

In this light we understand better why St John Eudes, St Margaret Mary Alacoque, St Alphonsus and others were so eager to promote the liturgical celebration of the feast of the Sacred Heart of Jesus. They all understood in their hearts that the eucharistic celebration is joyous thanksgiving and praise for the great love God has manifested to us in Jesus. Therefore, they saw that the mystery of the inexhaustible love of Jesus' heart is a special reason for joyful celebration. Not only did they want a special feast, but they intended to call people's attention to this joyful dimension of the mystery of redemption.

For one who truly venerates the Sacred Heart it is unthinkable to consider the Sunday Mass as a mere exercise of duty. Rather, it is an immeasurable privilege to be near to the Lord, to be assured of his coming to us in love. It is utter joy to join Christ so intimately in the praise of the Father.

This renewed liturgy is marked by this joyous praise of God, but this does not mean that we do not need special attention today to the love of Jesus' heart. Liturgy needs the joy that comes from the depths of our hearts, nourished by the heartfelt love of Jesus.

The pious Israelites joyfully sang their pilgrim-songs on the way to the Temple. How great, then, must our joy be when we experience in faith the ineffable love with which Jesus meets us in the Eucharist and in so many other saving signs of redemption! The dynamics of the life of the Church and of our life bring us closer to the Lord. This is our abiding and ever increasing joy. "How I rejoiced when they said to me, 'Let us go to the house of God' " (Ps 122:1).

This eucharistic, thankful and joyous love of Jesus transforms all our life into a cheerful pilgrimage to our eternal home, with the Lord leading us towards a trustful homecoming. Friendship with Jesus here on earth is both a "being with" and a "living in" Christ in a wholesome tension between the now and the not-yet. Christ has taken hold of us; he draws us closer to his heart. The incipient joy, great as it is, makes us look forward to its fulfilment when heart in heart forever reposes.

* * *

Why are you downcast, my soul, why do you sigh within me? In spite of my sinfulness and weaknesses I have enough reasons to be consoled, even to rejoice, for I can still praise you, my dearest Lord. It is right that I weep because of my sins, but it is more fitting to rejoice because even my past sins tell me to praise your merciful love with all my heart, for you have forgiven me. My pain for coming so late to love you is one more sign that you do not take your loving kindness away from me.

All creation and the whole history of salvation tell me of your great love for us. The joyful and serene countenance of people who love you tells me without words: learn to love Jesus, learn it better every day; and your heart will overflow with happiness and will radiate peace.

When I see priests and religious with sour faces, I feel I should ask them to go into hiding until they have again found joy in you, dear Lord. Help them to realize how absurd it is for those who know you to be disturbed by trifles and to be embittered by small offences. Compassionate Saviour, help them to seek and find all their joy in you.

Jesus, I thank you for having allowed me, many times in my life, to meet people who, in the midst of most painful suffering, radiate joy and peace and are a most convincing invitation to others to praise you. You offer your love as source of joy and peace to all who sincerely seek you. O Divine Physician, heal us all from self-provoked sadness. Let us drink joyfully from your springs of salvation!

Lord, let your countenance shine upon us! Send us your light and your truth. Make us wise enough to seek joy at the purest fountain, your heart.

We are thirsty for your love, and we come to you. Let us drink as you promised, so that streams of living water will flow from within us. Send us your Holy Spirit and make us joyous messengers of your blissful love!

28

The Heart of Jesus and the body of the redeemed

> "At his coming into the world, Jesus said: 'Sacrifice and offering thou didst not desire, but thou hast prepared a body for me. Whole-offerings and sin-offerings thou didst not delight in'. Then I said, 'Here am I: as it is written in the scroll, I have come, O God, to do thy will' " (Heb 10:5–7).

> " 'Destroy this temple', Jesus replied, 'and in three days I will raise it again'. They said, 'It has taken forty-six years to build this temple. Are you going to raise it again in three days?' But the temple he was speaking of was his body. After his resurrection his disciples recalled what he had said, and they believed the Scripture and the words that Jesus had spoken" (Jn 2:19–22).

AT the time Christ came into the world the great world religions, as well as the mainstreams of philosophy, showed great disdain for the human body. Early christianity had to face this problem. The biblical texts are strong and clear. Christ's true humanity, including the bodily dimension, belongs to the foundations of our faith. The dignity of the human body appears both in Christ's sacrifice on the cross and in his resurrection.

From the beginning Jesus praises the Father for his body; it is a gift of the Father. In his body Jesus is consecrated to do the Father's will. While the letter to the Hebrews emphasizes that the true body of Christ brings to an end all kinds of whole-offerings, in John's gospel Jesus himself sees in his body, which is to be offered for humankind, the real temple. The bodily reality has much to do with the "adoration of God in spirit and truth" (Jn 4:24).

True, "God is spirit", but he lets his glory shine in his visible works, of which the human body is his masterpiece, the embodiment of spirit. In his or her bodily reality the human person is to manifest visibly his or her being created to the image and likeness of God. In Jesus the body and, therefore, also the physical heart become absolutely privileged realities in the work of redemption.

On the cross Jesus reveals himself as embodied freedom in the act of supreme love and trust. He offers his life — "his body" in biblical language — as the greatest gift received from the Father and the greatest offering to be brought to the Father for humankind. At the hour of his death Jesus' body becomes the real temple wherein God is adored, and his loving heart is the "holiest of holies" in this temple.

In his battered body and his heart widely opened for us, Jesus makes visible and tangible his love for us and for his Father. Nailed to the cross, his arms reach out for all. This body and this heart build bridges between heaven and earth and between persons.

This crucified body is the acceptable sacrifice, not because of the bitter pains it has to suffer but for the love which shines through even in this cruel death. It is "the body which is given up for us", and Jesus wants to be sure that every believer throughout the ages will not only be reminded of this but will also come in contact with this body which is given up for him or her.

And after having served in the work of redemption, Jesus' body is not taken away. It is raised to glory and is the perennial gift to the Father and at the same time a gift to all believers. In his body Jesus has fullness of life, and while giving up this body for humankind he receives the greatest glory which shines in it eternally. So he can say: "I am the resurrection and I am life" (Jn 11:25).

We are "the body of Christ". This paradigm has rich and realistic meaning. We enter into the covenant between Christ and his Church with our full bodily reality: not only with intellect, memory and will but also with affections, sentiments, passions. All these dimensions are "embodied".

The body of Christ, having become the real "temple", the embodied "cult", embraces all of us. Not only are we an intimate part of Jesus' consecration prayer (cf. Jn 17), but in all our dimensions, and especially in our body, we are also consecrated in and through Christ's sacrificial body. "It is by the will of God that we have been consecrated through the offering of the body of Jesus Christ once and for all" (Heb 10: 10).

The human body is not just united with a soul; the person is spirited, the very expression and evidence of the spiritual dimension. The wounded, alienated person suffers all kinds of splits and dichotomies. The redeemed person is intact, having gained an integral wholeness. The devotion to the Sacred Heart of Jesus should be seen in this perspective. Cardinal Ratzinger, prefect of the Congregation for the Doctrine of Faith, points to it: "The theology of the body proposed by the encyclical *Haurietis Aquas* is an apologia of the heart, of the senses and sentiments".

In Jesus the integrated wholeness of body, soul and spirit has become love "made flesh". It is not enough to say that God has revealed his love through the body of Christ; his body itself is revelation of God's love.

For some time the devotion to the Sacred Heart was burdened by the unnecessary theory that the physical heart of Jesus is the seat of all his love. This theory was one of the main causes of the reluctance of the Holy See to approve any liturgical proposal that might be somehow marked by it. In his book *Novena to the Sacred Heart*, St Alphonsus rejected the theory and thus helped to remove obstacles. Already at that time he insisted on the enormous relevance of the human brain for the affective life. Yet the heart remains the basic symbol of embodied love, and in it all movements of affection and sentiment are really felt.

All parts of the holy scriptures, Old and New Testaments, make frequent use of this symbol, thereby attesting to the biblical emphasis on the bodily, visible, tangible realities. The "heart" is present even in the central beatitude, "How blest are those whose hearts are pure; they shall see God" (Mt 5: 8).

The truth that our body is a temple of God gives us an indispensable motive for a holy life, especially for watchfulness over intentions, affections and conduct. "Surely you know that you are God's temple, where the Spirit of God dwells. Anyone who destroys God's temple will himself be destroyed, because the temple of God is holy; and that temple you are" (1 Cor 3: 16–17). "Do you not know that your bodies are members of Christ?" (1 Cor 6: 15).

This vision applies not only to a christian view of chastity (1 Cor 6: 19) but to all our moral and religious life. Attention has to be given to the ordering of our affective life, which tangibly involves our heart but also is most decisive for all our desires, decisions and our conduct.

As Christians, then, we cannot separate man into spheres and parts, body and soul. And in the spontaneous devotion to the Sacred Heart, when we speak of the love of Jesus, we cannot abstract it from his bodily heart. The heart is always the symbol of the centre of one's being, and thus of wholeness and integration. The whole person is to become embodied love.

* * *

Most loving Saviour, from the beginning unto your last breath and heart-beat you considered and honoured your body as a gift of the Father. All your bodily life, and especially your sensitive heart, were praise of the Father. Your battered body was the most admirable prayer of total abandonment into the hands of the Father, a prayer for us.

Now we look up to your glorified body, yearning to find our beatitude in its splendour and to contemplate it through all eternity. We see your heart as the fountain of love for heaven and earth. Heaven has no need for a splendid temple; your body is the beauty that delights all the saints. Your heart is the holiest of holies in this eternal temple.

Your glorified body with this loving heart draws us to you. In it we have the firmest promise of eternal life. Help us, by the power of your Spirit, to honour our own and our neighbour's bodies as temples of the Holy Spirit, to be put totally into the service of adoring and serving love.

With great trust we look to your heart and ask you to illumine and strengthen us with your grace. Grant us the wisdom to use all the noble faculties of our souls and all the energies of our bodies in your service and for the benefit of the redeemed.

29

The Heart of Jesus and victory over godlessness

> "Knowing God, they have refused to honour him as God, or to render him thanks. Hence all their thinking has ended in futility, and their misguided minds are plunged in darkness. They boast of their wisdom, but they have made fools of themselves. . . Thus, because they have not seen fit to acknowledge God, he has given them up to their own depraved reason. This leads them to break all rules of conduct. They are filled with every kind of injustice, mischief, rapacity, and malice; they are one mass of envy, murder, rivalry, treachery, and malevolence; whisperers and scandal-mongers hateful to God, insolent, arrogant, and boastful . . . they show no loyalty to parents, no conscience, no fidelity to their plighted word; they are without natural affection and without pity" (Rom 1:21–22; 28–31).

THE devotion to the Sacred Heart of Jesus had a time of great flowering before and during the French Revolution, when influential parts of society in France and neighbouring countries turned away from faith in Christ. The veneration was understood as a call for merciful love in the face of disastrous aberrations. Today's situation is even more dramatic. Godlessness spreads in many forms.

On the existential level, man becomes godless when he severs himself from the love of God. He radicalizes this alienation when he also theoretically denies the God who is love. A society which is "heartless and without pity" is godless even before the existence of God is denied.

The most explicit and monstrous godlessness is organized dialectic atheism, which interprets history as being guided by the motor of growing class-conflict and class-hatred. It opposes this hate-filled interpretation to christian faith in God who has created man out of love and for love. Surely, this is a godlessness that is "heartless and without pity".

Within this aggressive form of atheism and along with it, there are many gods which sever man from God: self-glorification leading to explicit refusal to adore a personal God, arrogance, lust for power, terrorism, senseless arms race, merciless consumerism that works cruel injustices on the rest of humanity.

Add to this shocking picture the hidden atheism in the hearts and conduct of many people who call themselves Christians, while their thinking and life-style are contaminated and largely directed by practical and theoretical atheism.

Only living faith in the God of love, who has revealed himself in Jesus, can smash these false gods and unmask the various forms of godlessness. Only if our inmost being is filled with the message of love and its transforming grace, and if we turn wholeheartedly to this love which is symbolized in the heart of Jesus, can we protect our hearts and build in the world around us effective dams against the threatening flood of godlessness.

In the present world situation, christian faith calls more than ever for firm resolution, a radical option for the reign of love. We become credible witnesses insofar as this option takes hold of all our being, our thoughts, desires, affections, memory and will.

In his solemn prayer, in which he expresses his inmost heart, Jesus shows us the way to oppose godlessness in the world: "May they all be one: as thou, Father, art in me, and I in thee, so also may they be in us, that the world may believe that thou didst send me" (Jn 17:21). Jesus made known to his disciples the tender and strong love for which the Father sent him into the world. It is also in view of this mission, which he entrusts to us, that he wants to draw us to his heart and fill us with his love, so that we can bring it into the world. Jesus sends us out with and for the same love which he has revealed: "I made thy name known to them, and will make it known, so that the love thou hast for me may be in them, and I may be in them" (Jn 17:26).

We can offer this short definition of the scope of the devotion to the Sacred Heart: it is learning to love Jesus and to love with Jesus. This is what the world, threatened by lovelessness and godlessness, needs most urgently. Only a heart glowing with Christlike love can effectively repel all forms of hidden and open atheism. Only such a love can unmask all disguises of unbelief, and only the greatest love can find the remedies which humankind needs so desperately in this age of unbelief and godlessness.

At this time of crucial decisions of history, all who are captured by the heartfelt love of Christ must join hands and hearts for a common witness to faith bearing fruit in love and justice.

* * *

O heart full of love, O kindly light and fiery flame, you have come to heal the wounded world, and for this you "set fire to the earth and wish it were already kindled" (Lk 12: 49). But for this confused world you are also the sign which impels each of us to make our own choice. The decision which you desire and which you make possible by grace is for the reign of peace and salvation, the decision for faithful love, to the honour of the heavenly Father. Those who reject your love doom themselves to the reign of darkness, deception, hatred and enmity.

Lord, I yearn to decide firmly and forever to love you with all my heart, and I am ashamed that in the past I have often offended you by inconsistency and half-heartedness. Looking at your loving heart I begin to realize the greatness of this injustice. I see it as injustice to your love and majesty. If I love you with only half my heart, I have not yet really acknowledged you as my God. I see also now that it is a terrible injustice to humankind, which is so much in need of credible witnesses, people who show by their lives what it is to adore God.

O faithful Heart of Jesus, change us, enlighten and strengthen us in this time of separation. Help all Christians to join together in strong faith and faithful love, so that the world may believe and find the truth of life, the trust that an infinitely merciful God is concerned with fatherly love for all his creatures. O Lord, free the godless from their misery and emptiness.

Beloved Saviour, it is terrible to see that in spite of the alarming signs of the times so many Christians are apathetic and lazy. Awaken us all, fill us with new zeal and enthusiasm and show us the most effective ways to proclaim faith in you and in the heavenly Father.

30

The Heart of Jesus and our peace mission

> "Let Christ's peace be arbiter in your hearts; to this peace you were called as members of a single body. And be filled with gratitude. Let the message of Christ dwell among you in all its richness" (Col 3 : 15–16).

IN his encyclical *Haurietis Aquas* Pius XII gave the devotion to the Sacred Heart a programme of peace. "Let all who proudly call themselves Christians be fully committed to the kingdom of God on earth. Let them choose the devotion to the Heart of Jesus as a distinctive sign and source of unity, salvation and peace".

Configuration of the hearts of believers to the heart of Jesus proves authentic by the "fruits of the Spirit": "The harvest of the Spirit is love, joy, peace, patience, kindness, goodness, fidelity, gentleness and self-control" (Gal 5 : 22–23). "Love, joy and peace" are the heart of this rich harvest. All the other distinctive qualities of the redeemed are signs of a peaceful heart and the "armour" of peace-makers.

The first absolute condition for our peace-mission is that Christ's peace is "arbiter in our hearts". But the letter to the Colossians makes clear also that Christ's disciples see peace as a calling which concerns all members of a single body. We may think first of the Church as "body of Christ" but also of the whole of humankind for whom Christ died and is risen. As Christians, if we are grateful for the gift of peace and if the gospel of peace dwells in our hearts in all its richness, we will be committed to peace for everyone on earth.

Christ in person is our reconciliation and peace. In him the saving plan of God, the design for peace, is fulfilled and revealed. By consecration to the Heart of Jesus and by participating in the consecration of the world to the Sacred Heart, we experience in our inmost being what God tells us through the prophet: "I know the plans of my heart are plans for peace, not disaster, reserving a future full of hope for you" (Jer 29: 11).

But we cannot overlook the condition spelled out clearly: "When you seek me you shall find me, if you seek me with all your heart" (Jer 29: 13). We can call for peace and serve the cause of peace among all people only when our hearts are turned fully to God. This is precisly what devotion to the Sacred Heart intends. Turning to the heart of Jesus with a grateful heart means meeting the Redeemer of the world.

Whoever tastes the peace flowing from Jesus' heart will also experience that this very peace, the undeserved gift of the Redeemer, wants to be the arbiter in our hearts, telling us how we are to fulfil our calling to peace "as members of a single body".

The first response of a grateful heart to the gift of peace with God and of peace of heart will be a strong desire that all may rejoice in this same peace. Christ's faithful disciples will radiate peace, fulfilling the prophecy: "Streams of living water shall flow out from within him" (Jn 7: 38). Peace mission, in the first place, is a kind of "overflow of the peace-filled heart". But this alone does not suffice. Each of us, according to our charism, capacity and place, is meant to work as peace-maker with all our competence and endurance. Motivated by gratitude to do this, our hearts will be widened to receive an even greater portion of the messianic peace.

The most serious peace researchers of our time come to the insight that the commitment to peace is a long-term task, and the most decisive part of the task is forming peace-loving and peace-making persons and groups.

A theology of the heart of man, and especially of the heart of Jesus, comes to the same result but with even greater evidence and emphasis. Our first and most urgent contribution to the peace of the world is the configuration of our hearts with the heart of the "Prince of Peace" and his "thoughts of peace".

Those who believe in the beatitudes as saving rule in God's kingdom will be drawn powerfully to the heart of Jesus when they understand his promise: "How blest are the peacemakers; God shall call them his sons" (Mt 5: 9). By being wholly one with Christ and totally dedicated to his mission as reconciliator, we are sons and daughters with the only Son of God.

The blessing of the peace-makers is preceded by the blessing of "those whose hearts are pure; they shall see God" (Mt 5:8). Human hearts can be truly "pure" only when thoroughly filled with the all-embracing love of Jesus, for we are simply and thoroughly created and redeemed for that love. Unless we give it all the room in our heart and our will, impure kinds of love and desires will take over the rest.

The peace of Christ, which exults in our heart and is our only arbiter, has miraculous powers to build bridges from heart to heart and in human communities. This peace is given to all who "joyfully draw water from the springs of salvation". Thus gradually, through mutual help, we discover in ourselves and in others the inner resources that come from God. This renewed faith in the good in ourselves and others is indispensable for our peace mission.

From all this develops the eminent art of non-violent commitment to peace and to peaceful solutions of conflicts. This trust in our inner resources is recommended by the Apostle: "My friends, I have no doubt in my own mind that you yourselves are quite full of goodness and equipped with knowledge of every kind, well able to give advice to one another; I have written to refresh your memory" (Rom 15:14–15). But St Paul also points to the art of actually mobilizing these resources: "Never pay back evil for evil. Let your aims be such that all men count honourable. If possible, so far as it lies with you, live at peace with all men. . . If your enemy is hungry, feed him; if he is thirsty, give him a drink; by doing this you will heap live coals on his head. Do not let evil conquer you, but use good to defeat evil" (Rom 12:17–21).

The image of "heaping live coals on the head" needs explanation. It is taken from the experience of the housewife of ancient times who, after cooking, gathered the live coals at the head of the hearth so that fire never would be missing in the house. Thus, in our relations with our neighbour, especially with someone who causes us trouble, we discover and gather all our inner resources of goodness and let the other feel that, in spite of all difficulties, we believe that he, too, has resources for goodness and truth. This means "to speak truth in love" and thus serve the cause of peace in justice and justice in peace.

Non-violent action in every kind of conflict aims not at all to destroy the adversary. On the contrary, it is based on the trust that he can become a friend, a friend of truth, justice and peace. If our heart is firmly set on this course, we can hope that he will finally feel this appeal, this advance of trust. Such trust is authentic and efficacious if it is grounded in God.

The art of creative non-violence has to be learned and exercised in shared efforts. But most important is that the inner resources be constantly assured by "joyfully drawing water from the springs of salvation", from Christ, the Prince of peace, through the power of his Spirit.

Thereby, many people may first enter the road that leads to Christ before they come to explicit faith in Christ, due to their experience with peace-radiating and peace-making believers who reveal by their conduct the fountain of these inner resources, the "springs of salvation".

Everyone who is not mentally and morally insane should understand that, in the long run, not even a minimum of world peace can be guaranteed by endless armament races and mutual threats of annihilation through the "deterrent" of nuclear weapons. The longer this inhumane situation continues, the greater becomes the risk that what nobody wants will happen. Meanwhile, the reciprocal feelings of nations deteriorate greatly. Such a "deterrent" is already a beginning of destruction of one's own humanity and of the conditions for true reconciliation.

Decades ago wc heard frequently of "moral armament" and — thanks be to God — many gave that better armament high priority over military armament. But what we need is a firm peace-covenant, the preparation of which should have the highest priority from now on. And that requires more than mere moral re-armament.

Paul's letter to the Ephesians gives an idea of what is needed: "Find your strength in the Lord, in his mighty power. Put on all the armour which God provides. . . Take up God's armour; then you will be able to stand your ground when things are at their worst, to complete every task and still to stand. . . Let the shoes on your feet be the gospel of peace, to give you firm footing; and with these take up the great shield of faith, with which you will be able to quench all the flaming arrows of the evil one. Take salvation for helmet; for sword take that which the Spirit gives you — the words that come from God" (Eph 6:10–17).

In this perspective and with this spirit of the gospel of peace, nations should train in "re-armament" for forceful and just non-violence, for peaceful conflict-solutions, for mutual respect and trust. This has to be learned and prayed for on all levels, beginning with family life. Christians should be leaders in this approach, inspired by faith in the gospel of peace.

Surely "trans-armament" with and for non-violent commitment to justice and peace will also unmask injustice, hypocrisy, all forms of violence, but all these things should be done with the high art of truth in love, in shared search for a thoroughly humane peace.

* * *

We praise you, Father, Lord of heaven and earth, for having sent us your beloved Son Jesus Christ to be our reconciliation and our peace. We adore your "thoughts of peace" which you have revealed in Jesus.

We firmly believe that you intend to give us the fullness of your peace, since you have sent the One who, in Person, is Our Peace. We thank you for the experience of peace in our hearts and for our vocation to be peace-makers, thus to prove us to be truly your children. We thank you also for having given us, in our age, men and women who radiate peace and are wholly dedicated to the cause of peace and reconciliation.

Merciful Father, in the name of Jesus we implore you to forgive us our many sins against peace and our negligences in fostering it. Grant us, as sign of your forgiveness, a burning zeal and constant faithfulness in promoting its causes in our hearts, in our families and communities, in our church and in the whole of christianity. Let there be peace among nations in justice and mutual respect.

O heart of our Redeemer, fountain of salvation and love, you have consecrated yourself totally to peace, to the glory of your Father and for our salvavtion. We want to consecrate ourselves anew and with you for the cause of peace. For when you consecrated yourself before your death, you took us, your disciples, into that all-embracing consecration. Lord, accept our renewed consecration, grant us your Spirit so that we may be consecrated in truth and all our life may bear fruit in love, joy and peace. Amen.